CW00544620

Nineteenth Century Bath
Architects & Architecture

NEIL JACKSON

Nineteenth Century Bath
Architects & Architecture

Foreword by
SIR HUGH CASSON

ASHGROVE PRESS, BATH

First published in Great Britain by
ASHGROVE PRESS LIMITED
4 Brassmill Centre, Brassmill Lane
Bath, Avon BA1 3JN

© Neil Jackson 1991

ISBN 1 85398 016 1

First published 1991

Photoset in 11pt Palatino by
Ann Buchan (Typesetters), Middlesex
Printed and bound in Great Britain by
Dotesios Limited, Trowbridge
Wiltshire

For my parents, who first brought me to Bath
and
for their granddaughter who was born there

CONTENTS

ACKNOWLEDGEMENTS

The publication of this book would not have been possible without the help of two generous awards. The first, which assisted with the initial research, was a Royal Institute of British Architects Gordon Ricketts Bursary, given in 1982. The second, seven years later, was a research award given by the Architects Registration Council of the United Kingdom. This made possible the inclusion of the illustrations which are so much part of the book. I am grateful to the Royal Institute for their initial enthusiasm and their lasting patience during the long gestation of this project, and to the Registration Council for their renewed expression of faith in my endeavours.

I am also grateful to a number of individuals and institutions for allowing me to use illustrative material held in their collections: The Ashmolean Museum, Oxford; Stephen Baker; The Bath Reference Library, County of Avon; The British Architectural Library, RIBA, London; The Conway Library, The Courtauld Institute of Art, London; Hugh Crallan; Gerald Deacon; The Guildhall Library, City of London; The Lady Lever Art Gallery, Port Sunlight; The National Gallery, London; The Polytechnic of the South Bank, London; Prior Park College, Bath; The Royal Commission on Historic Monuments, London; The Somerset Archaeological and Natural History Society, Taunton; Sir John Summerson; The Trustees of Sir John Soane's Museum, London.

As with projects such as this, it has been necessary to seek help, advice and support from a great many people. Jim Denning of Avebury Publishing first encouraged me to write the book but it was Robin Campbell and Ashgrove Press who eventually brought it into the light. Francis Kelly, Tim Mowl, Julian Orbach and Tony Walter read early versions of parts or all of the text and provided me with copious comments which improved an otherwise ill-considered manuscript. David McLaughlin and Rosemary Northcote drew my attention to much of the nineteenth century architecture of Bath in the early days of the Victorian Society's

Avon Group, a venture so keenly supported by Hermione Hobhouse. More recently, James Elliott and Dennys Hinton lent their support and Sir Hugh Casson provided the *Foreword*. Without their efforts, this book would have been, quite literally, far thinner.

Over the years, a number of sources have been plundered in the hope of finding relevant and useful material. Central to my enquiries has been the Bath Reference Library, and the librarian and her staff have been endlessly accommodating. When Alan Crozier-Cole's office archives (which went back to James Wilson c 1840) were deposited at the British Architectural Library Drawings Collection another source became particularly relevant, and another curator and staff proved exceedingly helpful. Meanwhile the special collection at the Polytechnic of the South Bank provided, under the expert supervision of John Thomas, an immediate and resourceful facility at my place of employment. Elsewhere, Gerald Deacon and Sir John Summerson were kind enough to share their collections with me. Cannon J J Kelly allowed me access to the records held at St John the Divine Roman Catholic Church. Even before this project became a book, James Lees-Milne had entertained me in the rooms where William Beckford had lived and, like Sydney Blackmore, had shared with me his enthusiasm for H E Goodridge. Richard Emerson of the National Monuments Record for Scotland had also provided illustrations of Goodridge's work for the Duke of Hamilton. More recently, Belinda Carruthers and the late Major W F Eyre spared me the time to discuss their family chapel at the Perrymead Cemetery and D Dent Young showed me the Cloisters nearby. And all the while, countless people opened their doors to seemingly bizarre enquiries – do your stair balusters look like this? or, do you mind if I stand on your balcony to measure the front of your house? or, can I use your bedroom window to photograph that tall building over there? These unknown people were always so accommodating.

The first draft of the book was typed from my manuscript by Barbara Cottee: the second was put onto computer by Nancy Sullivan, using facilities generously made available at Kansas State University. That was many years ago but their effort has not been forgotten. Subsequent and final drafts were prepared on equipment provided by the University of Bath: here I need to thank Lyn Norris at the Computer Centre, and John Harlow and Mark Harding of the Small Systems Unit for their time and interest.

ACKNOWLEDGEMENTS

Scott Morrison and Martin Winson laboured under hot photographic lamps at the Bath Reference Library: they have reproduced many of the illustrations garnered from that excellent source. In addition, Scott Morrison printed over one hundred of my own photographs which I included in the text: he also printed a great many more I did not use.

In the end it was my father whose constant support and encouragement persuaded me not to resign the boxes of photographs and computer print-out to some high and dusty shelf. As the *Dedication* shows, he first brought me to Bath, but he also allowed me to bring Bath to him.

1 St John the Divine, South Parade by Charles Francis Hansom, 1861

FOREWORD
by

Sir Hugh Casson
CH, KCVO, PPRA, RDI, RIBA

Bath must be one of the most described cities in Europe. Yet most of the descriptions read as if a glass dome had been popped over the place in 1800 and nothing had happened to it since. The aim of this seriously researched and affectionately written book is to redress the balance – to remind us that no city can escape the rattling wheels of architectural fashion trundling down its streets, even if the vestments of stone or slate in which most of Bath's buildings are clad try to conceal the fact. All the styles are here, from Palladian to Picturesquen from Italianate (for villas) to High Gothic (for churches) and secular Gothic (for schools and railway stations). Many famous nineteenth century architects – Loudon, Street, Gilbert Scott and Brydon – worked here but it is nice to read of so many excellent architects dragged out of undeserved obscurity: John Pinch, the master of the terrace on the sloping site; H E Goodridge, protegé of Beckford; J J Scoles, designer of Napoleonically-scaled St Paul's at Prior Park; Edward Davis, the architect of the Royal Victoria Park and that remarkable City Architect Major Davis, the discoverer and restorer of the Roman Baths and architect of one of Bath's most conspicuous buildings, The Empire Hotel (1899–1901).

Bath is indeed a lucky city – lucky in its setting and its architecture, lucky in its comparative immunity from rapacious entrepreneurs, well-meaning councillors and insensitive architects – lucky too in finding in the author of this enjoyable book so perceptive a recorder of the city's less celebrated treasures.

2 The Empire Hotel and Parade Gardens   by Charles Edward Davis, 1899

INTRODUCTION

On Tuesday 18 July 1989 *The Bath and West Evening Chronicle* carried a front-page column headed 'Empire's Status Listed' [2]. So the Empire Hotel, completed in the year Queen Victoria died, has become a Grade II Listed Building! That very piece of news made me wonder if this whole book was redundant, not because its argument was futile but because its effort was now unnecessary, for it might be seen as preaching to the converted. But I think not. That piece of news must have been met, in places, by raised eyebrows and gasps of incredulity – but more likely by resigned indifference. The Empire Hotel, like its giant neighbour, the Abbey, must be amongst the most misunderstood architecture in the city: which is where this book tries to help.

Bath is a city of confused identities. On driving in from the motorway the first indication of the city is a sign which says *Welcome to Bath – the Roman City*; and then shortly after another, this one bearing a crest, proclaims *Bath – the Georgian City*. Thus, juggling contradictory images, perhaps of Julius Caesar and Jane Austen, the visitor prepares for the waters which have drawn people here over so many centuries. Meanwhile, outside the Pump Room ballroom, a man in knee-breeches and a powdered wig is playing eighteenth-century music on the recorder while the open-topped buses trundle around the congested streets drawing attention to the absurdities of the Empire Hotel where the roofline, we hear, reflects the status of the lords, gentlemen and commonfolk who stay there. How Bath is still misunderstood!

This book is not intended as an architectural history: it is neither total nor definitive in its coverage of the nineteenth-century buildings of Bath. It hazards guesses and makes assessments. It is, without doubt, subjective in its choice of buildings and the comments it makes. But it does try to be intelligent about it, and only my readers can assess whether it is successful.

This book sets out to explain the nineteenth-century buildings of Bath. It tries to put them in their national context and thus justify their appearance. It offers an exercise in analysis which could be applied to Oxford or Glasgow or any city which bears the impress of nineteenth-century growth. In this case, it just happens to be Bath.

But the choice of Bath is made knowingly. For where else in Britain is a city so well known for what it is not? It does not take an expert eye to tell that the statues of emperors and generals which surround the Great Bath could hardly be Roman: and a careful eye can soon detect that the windows of the *piano nobile* in the King's Circus and Royal Crescent have at some time been altered. But no casual observer will be able to tell that much of the fan vaulting of the Abbey is only a little over a century old, or that the battlemented south aisle, overlooking Abbey Churchyard, dates from 1923 – two years before Walter Gropius built the Bauhaus. And did that man who charmed us with his recorder realize what an anachronism he really was, since his costume predated his backdrop by about a hundred years? What is this city that we see, and in which some of us live? Is it really a 'Georgian' city, preserved for ever in some architectural aspic?

No, of course, it is not. Bath, today, is a twentieth-century city and we should regard it as such. We should regard it with the same respect which the nineteenth-century architects did but, like them, we should not be cowed by it. Although often constrained to Bath stone and Welsh slate, the architects of nineteenth-century Bath rarely worked within the comfortable confines of the Palladian tradition. Like William Wilkins at the Lower Assembly Rooms, they were stylistically innovative and sometimes, like Sir Gilbert Scott at St Andrew's Church, which loomed to 240 feet behind the Royal Crescent before the air-raids took it, they were overtly challenging. New building types provided justification for new materials – laminated timber at Bath Spa and cast iron at Green Park stations – and new attitudes provided opportunities for fresh solutions – Roman Catholic emancipation at Charles Francis Hansom's St John the Divine, and scientific interment at John Claudius Loudon's Abbey Cemetery.

In explaining the buildings of nineteenth-century Bath this book attempts to remove some of the mystique which has enshrouded the city for so long, to convert carbuncles into carats and to show that change is not such a bad thing after all. Bath needs good modern architecture as much today as it did during the nineteenth century. By understanding how it was done then, we might gain some insight into how to do it now.

Neil Jackson
Cavendish Place, Bath
September 1989

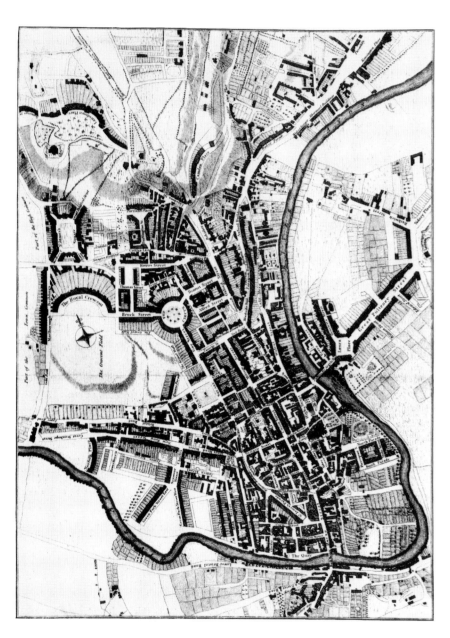

3 Plan of Bath   Charles Harcourt Masters and William Hibbert's plan of 1801
shows the extent of the City of Bath as the nineteenth century began.

CHAPTER 1

Continuity and Change

Georgian Bath is not what it might appear to be. It was not a planned city. It developed in a piecemeal fashion throughout the eighteenth century, largely as the product of the speculative ventures of both the Corporation and a number of individuals whose memory remains recorded in the street nomenclatures today: Gay, Milsom, Pulteney, Trymme, Wood and others [3]. Its cohesion was the result of a common building material, Bath stone, and a common architectural vocabulary, late-Renaissance Classicism.

Within this varied framework, Palladian or Adamesque, small groupings of planned development did occur. The most noticeable are those of the elder John Wood, his earliest development starting with his partly realised scheme for a Royal Forum to the east of the Abbey and his Queen Square to the north-west, this one culminating with the King's Circus* and Royal Crescent beyond. Here is found one of the great showpieces of European architecture. Yet how much of this is generally understood? The common analysis tends to relate the King's Circus to antique monuments such as the Colosseum in Rome, where the Orders are stacked up in a way which reflects their visual weight – Doric at the bottom, Ionic in the middle and Corinthian at the top – and so it is at the King's Circus [4]. But it was also that way in earlier, pre-Palladian buildings in Bath, such as the broadfronted no. 14 Westgate Street [5]. Even so, Sir John Summerson, writing in *Architecture in Britain 1530–1830* finds the King's Circus 'quaintly beautiful – as if some simple minded community had taken over an antique monument and neatly adapted it as a residence'. One suspects that he finds the Colosseum analysis too simplistic.

Examination of Wood's own writings indicate a deeper

*Now known just as 'The Circus'.

4 The King's Circus Only a careful eye can detect that the façade of the King's Circus has been substantially altered since it was built by the elder John Wood in 1754.

5 14 Westgate Street The vertical stacking of the Doric, Ionic and Corinthian Orders at 14 Westgate Street provides a precedent for John Wood's better known example at the King's Circus.

meaning and significance in his architecture than is generally appreciated. One interpretation is suggested by R S Neale in *Bath, 1680–1850, A Social History* and another is convincingly argued by Tim Mowl and Brian Earnshaw in *John Wood, Architect of Obsession*. In their discussion of the King's Circus and the Royal Crescent Mowl and Earnshaw present the hypothesis that these two great set pieces were intended by Wood to reflect, in their circle and crescent forms, prehistoric shrines to Bel and Onca, the sun and the moon gods. And, despite later attributions, it would appear likely that both pieces were built in the shapes originally planned by the elder Wood, although only one elevation, that of the King's Circus, was built to his design. Mowl and Earnshaw point out that in Tobias Smollett's *Expedition of Humphry Clinker* the King's Circus and the Royal Crescent are described as being by the same architect: and Smollett knew John Wood. Smollett also has Matthew Bramble refer to the King's Circus as 'a pretty bauble; contrived for show'. Is this just a sardonic comment, or was something special intended to be displayed – was the King's Circus knowingly *contrived*?

It is not my intention here to attempt an analysis of Wood's druidical designs at Bath but more to question how much of this eighteenth-century architecture is taken for granted. In an effort to further a strictly architectural analysis, it should be pointed out, as Neale does, that both Queen Square and the Circus were designed as inward-looking entities. In his *Description of Bath*, the elder Wood described the square thus:

> I preferred an inclosed Square to an open one, to make this as useful as possible: For the Intention of a Square in a City is for People to assemble together; and the Spot whereon they meet, ought to be separated from the Ground common to Men and Beasts, and even to Mankind in General, if Decency and good Order are necessary to be observed in such Places of Assembly; of which I think, there can be no doubt.

What was commenced here at Queen Square in 1728 was taken to its logical conclusion at the King's Circus in 1754. Here the sense of enclosure and structure was to be absolute. There was, in fact, not one circle but two; the outer circle of buildings enclosed an inner circle, a paved area devoid of all planting as John Robert Cozen's well-known drawing of 1773 shows. Here the outside world was excluded and the eye drawn irresistably inwards and then across towards the tiered structure of the encompassing buildings. At no point, on entering the King's Circus, could the visitor see beyond the enclosure, for by planning it in three equal segments, Wood had avoided any possible through-vistas.

It was in fact his son, the younger John Wood, who did more than anyone to upset the sense of utopia which his father had instigated. It is only because he followed his father's foundations so carefully that any sense of homogeneity exists within their work. Confusion of attribution, due to the use of the same name, the same style and the same building material has blurred the boundaries further. In his broadly Neo-Classical treatment of the Royal Crescent, the younger Wood made an architectural statement that is quite at odds with what his father had done in an older, Inigo Jones-inspired Palladianism at Queen Square and the King's Circus. Furthermore, whereas the King's Circus had been rich with references and iced with iconography, the Royal Crescent was bland almost to the point of boredom. Giant Order

Ionic columns rattle repetitively across its facade, hiccoughing in the centre where paired columns flank a thin, round headed window. Here there is none of the richness which the King's Circus displays. Indeed, the younger Wood, described by Mowl and Earnshaw as 'desperately solemn', seems to have avoided all attempt at elaboration wherever possible. The Royal Crescent is devoid of decoration and those parts of the King's Circus which were left to his attention, the windows for instance, are equally without feeling. So, in appraising the Royal Crescent, one is forced to consider its form as an outward expression, rather than an enclosing gesture. After all, it is a semi-ellipse rather than a semi-circle, flatter in the middle than the end; and in the conditions of the land lease which the younger Wood drew up with Sir Benet Garrard, the landowner was actually prevented by the architect not only from building in front of the Crescent, but even from planting trees there – thus maintaining the outlook from the Crescent. It is worth wondering whether the elder Wood would have had it this way. Would he not have sought a greater sense of enclosure: perhaps to maintain a sense of 'Decency and good Order', but more probably to help direct attention to the detail with which he would surely have covered his edifice?

The extent to which the younger Wood really failed to maintain his father's sense of control comes home in the incoherent arrangement of streets and buildings to the north east of the King's Circus. Here Bennett Street climbs shakily up the hill only to collide inconclusively with Lansdown Road. To the south the New Assembly Rooms faced directly onto the rear of the King's Circus. It is hard to see why Wood, given the awkward location of the site, did not make a more convincing attempt to relate the building either to Alfred Street to the south or to Bennett Street, with Russell Street coming in perpendicularly from the north. But the younger Wood seems to have been an unimaginative architect – Brock Street lacks any real inspiration and only works as a muted umbilical between the King's Circus and the Royal Crescent. Yet his work here is safely Palladian and thoroughly conservative: no wonder his father's more extraordinary ideas have been largely overlooked.

If the younger Wood failed to fathom his father's architecture, what remains today makes it no more easy a task for us. The King's Circus has lost the hardness of edge which Cozen depicted: the plane trees planted in the centre, when viewed from the far west end of Brock Street, appear to be but a continuation of the park to the south. What we see in the King's Circus and the Royal Crescent, and along Gay Street and Brock Street is in reality, a nineteenth-century interpretation. Certainly the architecture is the Woods', but the effect of the architecture within the space is much as the nineteenth century left it. Entry porch extensions stud the façades along Brock Street – some still black with nineteenth-century dirt – and throughout the development, as throughout the city, window proportions and glazing patterns have been changed, thus totally imbalancing the intended dimensional ratios within each elevation.

Perhaps in the interests of light and hygiene or, more likely, fashion, whole blocks of houses had their *piano nobile* windows transformed. The sill bands were removed and the sill levels were dropped, so that the proportions changed from about 1:1.5 to 1:2, and the reveals were chamfered. Cheap Patent Plate glass, first introduced in 1838, was fitted into the new sashes and the tiresome glazing bars were done away with. Encouraged, perhaps, by the repeal of the Glass Tax in 1845, owners needed no longer to look out onto cobbled streets from behind square-revealed sashes divided into twelve small panes, but now the greening streetscape could be generously surveyed through the breadth of Patent Plate glass. The effect, externally, was to change the impression from one of snug enclosure to rather cold exposure. Relatively few houses have survived this defacing (although no. 1 Royal Crescent has recently been returned to its original form). No. 16 Gay Street [6], however, retains its original sill band and reveals at *piano nobile* level. Although it is here shown with Patent Plate glazing, it presents nevertheless a far more contained elevation than its neighbours at nos. 15 and 17. An inspection of those façades, and others, will reveal the scars of the old sill bands.

About the time of the younger Wood's death in 1781, the initiative moved to architects who sought their inspiration not so much from Andrea Palladio, but from Robert Adam. Indeed, Adam himself prepared plans for a number of buildings in Bath, but only that for Pulteney Bridge was executed.

There is a lightness and delicacy about the Adamesque architecture of Bath which cannot be found in the earlier Palladian buildings. This is most noticeable in the work of Thomas Baldwin, whose designs in this manner, particularly the Guildhall (1776), Northumberland Buildings (c1780) and the Great Pump Room (1791), best express the later Georgian buildings of Bath. John Palmer, his successor in the post of City Architect, also built in this

6 15–17 Gay Street The staggered terraces of Gay Street were built in 1756–60. Later alterations to the *piano nobile* windows of Nos. 15 and 17 have served to change the whole proportional balance of the façade.

manner, but with a thinness which is really only redeemed by the spectacular meandering in the plan of his most dramatic composition, Lansdown Crescent (1789) [7]. Should Norfolk Crescent (c1798) be his, as Walter Ison suggests it is in *The Georgian Buildings of Bath*, then it represents a sad and spiritless counterpart to his earlier work in the upper town.

By the end of the eighteenth century the enforced domination of any one style had gone, to be replaced by a desire on the part of the

7 Lansdown Crescent The magnificent sweep of John Palmer's Lansdown Crescent of 1789 hides its overall thinness. William Beckford lived at No. 20, behind the bay window, and in the early 1820s had H E Goodridge build the bridge over to his house in Lansdown Place West.

architects to work in a number of styles. Indeed, John Eveleigh, who gave the Adamesque pediment on Somerset Place an almost Baroque flair, advertised himself in 1790 as being willing to prepare 'Designs for Mansions, Villas, Dwellings, etc. in the Gothick or modern taste'. Meanwhile, Palmer was also building Gothick, something even both the Woods had dabbled in. Eighteenth-century Bath had been dominated first by the Palladian and then by the Adam style, both supposedly Roman in origin, but the new century ushered in new styles, each drawn from new sources. It ushered in new architects too, for whereas eighteenth-century Bath was unique for being built, with the exception of Pulteney Bridge, by resident architects, nineteenth-century Bath is noticeable for the number of visiting architects it entertained.

There was really nothing very surprising in this. The needs of the city were changing: a super-abundance of residential accommodation was now available and what more was needed could soon be run up by local builders working within a firmly established tradition – and all the while, the dissemination of ideas was quickening. It is in the independent designs, the churches, public buildings and occasional houses that the work of the 'foreign' architects can be found. Thus Bath opened itself up to a variety of influences and styles in a century which was remarkable for just that. Change was almost constant, and where the older eighteenth-century properties did not match up, soon they too would be brought into line. Yet despite the departure from a common style, the continued use of that common building material, Bath stone, allowed the cohesion of the eighteenth-century city to remain.

CHAPTER 2

The End of Palladianism

The one local architect who was most successful in the early years of the nineteenth century was John Pinch. In his designs for terraces on Bathwick and Lansdown can be seen the final throes of the great eighteenth-century tradition, brought to a new height of elegance and refinement, and now infused with fresh references and meaning.

Following an earlier bankruptcy, it was in his capacity as surveyor to the Darlington Estates in the new suburb of Bathwick that Pinch first came to prominence. This development had been started by Thomas Baldwin in 1788, but the financial crisis of 1793, and the resulting collapse of the Bath City Bank, had led to his bankruptcy. Although Baldwin returned to work privately as an architect and speculator, Pinch took over responsibilities for the estate.

Pinch did not have the advantage of the broad urban vista, such as Great Pulteney Street, to redeem his architecture. Indeed, his sloping sites, as at New Sydney Place and Raby Place, could be thought of as distinctly disadvantageous. But he imparted to his architecture a vivacity rarely displayed by Baldwin and, like Baldwin, an imagery quite alien to that of the eighteenth-century terraces.

In his first terrace in Bathwick, New Sydney Place (1808) [8], Pinch employed an elevational arrangement very similar to Baldwin's central block on the south side of Great Pulteney Street, between William Street and Edward Street. This consisted of round-headed door and window openings forming an arcade at *piano rustica* level, a plain *piano nobile* and a frieze and continuous sill band below the mezzanine at second floor level. This arrangement is unremarkable; Robert Adam had used much the

8 New Sydney Place John Pinch built New Sydney Place in 1808 after replacing Thomas Baldwin as the Surveyor to the Darlington Estates. The similarity of this elevation to Baldwin's buildings along Great Pulteney Street indicates the influence of the latter.

9 Fitzroy Square, London In Fitzroy Square Robert Adam introduced, in 1790–95, a strong and cleanly expressed attic storey above the cornice, much as John Pinch was to do some fifteen years later in Bath.

same arrangement in Fitzroy Square, London (1790–95) [9]
contemporaneously with Baldwin. But Pinch and Adam both
introduced a strongly expressed attic storey above the cornice
where Baldwin had used but a balustrade, thus producing rather
more severe elevations.

New Sydney Place can be seen as a link with the past, a
continuation of a tradition, in its reference to Baldwin's work, as
well as an indicator of things to come. As this, it is both successful
and unsuccessful.

Its success is apparent in the way it addresses the slope of the
site. Hitherto, all stepped terraces in Bath – and there were quite a
number – were treated as individual or grouped units. The Woods'
houses in Gay Street (1756–60) step up regularly, each symmetrical
but unrelated to its neighbour; and the same is apparent at
Belmont (1768–73) and in the streets surrounding the New
Assembly Rooms. Here the buildings simply follow the lie of the
land, stepping up when it climbs and then levelling out on the flat.
Thus cornices and string courses break and break again in an
irregular, *stocatto* fashion providing no continuity or harmony
along the line of the street. The effect is of a city after an
earthquake: some buildings have slipped and some have not.

At New Sydney Place, no such irregularity is apparent. Pinch
seized upon his sloping site and used it to good effect. Whereas
each building steps up in a regular fashion, Pinch did not allow the
harmony and the continuity of the façade to be interrupted. Each
horizontal band of architectural decoration is given a twist at its
upper end, to bring it to the level of that at the next house [10]. This

10 New Sydney Place, Pompeian or Vitruvian scrollwork   The upward stepping of each house at New Sydney Place is reflected in the movement of the
string courses. See [18].

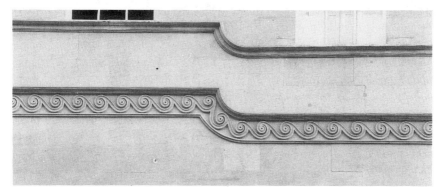

idea of ramped cornices was derived from early eighteenth-century panelling and stair strings and had been used in Bath before, such as in the elevations of Barnton Buildings built in 1768 and probably by the younger Wood. At New Sydney Place the effect is delightful and harmonises well with the rounded forms of the arcaded *piano rustica* and the flowing, Pompeian scrollwork within the friezes. In thus linking the façade, and refraining from emphasising the central window of each house, as earlier architects would have done in the Palladian manner, Pinch provides a unified frontage, which justifies, to some extent, the central, pedimented bay and the end pavilions.

Pinch used this successful method of linkage in at least two other instances. Before work finished on New Sydney Place, he started another hillside terrace, Cavendish Place, up on Lansdown, and in 1825 he returned to Bathwick to build a group of smaller houses, Raby Place [11]. Finally, there is St Mary's Buildings, which climb up Beechen Cliff from the Wells Road [12]. Although more humble than Raby Place, they have finesse and

11 Raby Place   Although a comparatively modest terrace, Raby Place, built in 1825 by John Pinch, addresses the sloping site in the same way as New Sydney Place and Cavendish Place had done earlier.

dignity that would suggest the hand of an accomplished architect. These buildings rise steeply and so the linking curves of the cornice and string course move upward in great rounded sweeps. The façades are otherwise almost devoid of ornamentation, but for the rounded door and window heads in the *piano rustica* and the subtle introduction of three sets of triglyphs, indicative of the Doric Order, below the cornice of each house. The steepness of the site and the pronounced curve of the cornice and string course make further ornamentation unnecessary. Since apparently no other nineteenth-century architect treated stepped terraces in this manner, it is not unlikely, as Charles Robertson has suggested in *Bath, An Architectural Guide*, that these buildings are by John Pinch. The restrained dignity of their facades would tend to confirm this.

Returning to New Sydney Place, the less successful aspect of the composition should now be considered. After 1728, when the elder John Wood built the north side of Queen Square, there was a tradition in urban terraced architecture of what can be best

12 St Mary's Buildings   Could St Mary's Buildings, hidden from view above the Wells Road, be by John Pinch? No other architect treated a hillside site in quite the same way.

13 Hanover Terrace, Regent's Park, London   In 1821–30 John Nash provided, at Hanover Terrace, the perfect expression of the palace façade.

referred to as the 'palace façade'. The idea was to build a large, unified façade, with central and corner accents, which would address an open space, usually private gardens.

Although comprised of any number of individual houses, the overall impression would be of one grand, palatial building, often of enormous pretension, and always larger than any one of their inhabitants could afford. In Bath, almost all the larger terraces allude to this intention: consider the Royal Crescent and Lansdown Crescent, or Camden Crescent and Somerset Place, neither of which were, in fact, completed. Outside Bath, the best examples can be found in London, where John Nash's metropolitan development of 1811–35 used palace façades almost *ad nauseam*. The imposing blocks which flank Regent's Park – Hanover Terrace [13], Cornwall Terrace and Cumberland Terrace in particular – with their mews, lodges and gates, aspire to a grandeur never realised in Bath. They address not a garden or a square, but a vast park, each a Blenheim or Stowe in its own right. They were emulating what Prior Park, at Bath, achieved. Nash took this theme to its final and ironic conclusion at Carlton House Terrace, overlooking the Mall. In 1827 Carlton House, the real urban palace, was demolished to be replaced by the urban terrace with the palace façade.

John Pinch's use of the palace façade at New Sydney Place is inappropriate. The sloping site does not suit a palace façade, even though it addresses Sydney Gardens, and the architecture itself is strong enough to survive without the pronounced central and end pedimented bays. The strength of the architecture is in its linked horizontal courses and the sense of verticality required is provided by the stepping of the houses as they rise up the hill. The rounded corner at the lower end is not so much a palatial end-accent, but a highly successful architectural device to bring the building around the corner: the elder John Wood did just this at no. 41 Gay Street. And it could also serve a role as a foil or book-end, to stop the building running down the hill.

In this respect Cavendish Place, which is not treated as a palace façade, is more successful, and in a way more honest. It is difficult, when the individual houses are so pronounced, to incorporate them into one convincing, uniform façade. Here Pinch seems to recognise this and treats the houses for what they are – a series of individual, but linked houses, climbing a steep hillside. Thus nos. 4 to 13 have a cohesion which the Woods' climbing terraces never achieved. The weakness of the terrace is at the ends. At its higher end the run of houses appears to stop in mid-flight, perhaps thwarted by Cavendish Villa (even though a cornice does return along this north face of no. 13), and at the lower end the terrace runs quite inconclusively into Park Place. Indeed, nos. 1, 2 and 3 Cavendish Place do not seem to belong to the terrace at all. Whereas it might have been his intention to continue the terrace uphill, terminating it in some visual book-end or, perhaps, a return, he should not have been allowed to leave the lower end so ill-thought out.

Honesty of expression and the palace façade come together in perfect harmony at Sion Hill Place [14], which Pinch built high up on Lansdown in 1817–20. In Wood's first palace façade on the north side of Queen Square, everything, in the relationship between elevation and plan, was what it seemed. The central house encompassed the five bays beneath the pediment, the centrally placed door flanked on each side by a pair of windows. Beyond this, two windows and a door identified the location of the adjacent houses. But as the eighteenth century progressed and the palace façade became *de rigueur* for Bath terraces, honesty and convenience in planning were sacrificed for the greater effect of the elevation. This is, of course, difficult to see: should one be able to spot this from the street, then the architect has failed in his intention. But tell-tale signs such as party walls and chimneys, later paintwork and even matching curtains in the windows, gave the lie to the appearance. In Thomas Baldwin's Sydney Place (1792)

14 Sion Hill Place   Built in 1817–20, Sion Hill Place is the best arranged of John Pinch's terraces.

it is clear that the central, pedimented bay contains two houses: what is not so immediately recognisable is that these houses are both of three bays' width, stealing a bay from each of the adjacent houses. A similar instance arises on the pedimented south side of St James Square, built by John Palmer between 1790 and 1793. Until recently the painting of the ashlar of no. 12 had made the architectural incongruities all too obvious.

At Sion Hill Place no such irregularities appear. The central pedimented bay contains one house and is set slightly proud. It is a weak feature in comparison to the great rounded bows of the houses at either end but, in having three windows, is stronger than the flanking houses with their paired windows. Pinch treats this elevation with the utmost honesty, for each house is clearly distinguishable. A discreet rhythm is set up in the solid and void of the façade: the windows of any one house are just a little closer together than those of any two adjacent houses. This gives the architect space to break the vertical line by offsetting the doors and windows in the rusticated *piano rustica* level without disturbing the overall regularity. Yet through all this the elevation works as one, and the concept of the palace façade is successfully exploited.

There are five major terraces thought to be built by John Pinch in the first quarter of the nineteenth century – New Sydney Place, Cavendish Place, Cavendish Crescent, Sion Hill Place and Raby Place – although some of the attributions are not wholly confirmed. It would seem likely, however, that they are the work of the same hand, and this despite the fact that the street directories for these years record a number of architects practising in the city: it is only John Pinch's name which appears regularly – 1800, 1805, 1809, 1813 and 1819, this last with his son. There was nothing to stop other architects picking up the influence of Baldwin and adopting Pinch's manner, but since these five buildings form such a coherent group chronologically, geographically and stylistically, there must have been one controlling hand. John Pinch died in 1827 and after that date no more elegant terraces such as these were built.

These five terraces effectively bring the theme of the terraced house into the nineteenth century but at the same time adorn it with a new-found gentility, derived from antiquity. When considered together, they can be seen to follow a fairly well defined pattern.

For most of the eighteenth century the terraced houses of Bath were limited above ground to three storeys in the main façade, and a fourth within the roof. This was, visually, a comfortable arrangement: the *piano rustica*, perhaps rusticated, was pronounced and solid; the *piano nobile*, often with the mezzanine storey above, was set between podium and entablature, and bore Giant Order columns or pilasters; and above the entablature was the pediment, flanked by a balustrade or blocking course, behind which the dormer windows of the third floor garret could be seen peeping. This was the Palladian arrangement.

Thomas Baldwin was probably the first person to extend this main façade to four floorss by expressing the attic as a solid element. At Northumberland Buildings (1778) [15] an extra storey is introduced above the level of the entablature and pediments,

15 Northumberland Buildings Northumberland Buildings, built by Thomas Baldwin in 1778, was a speculative venture and achieved maximum saleable space by introducing a full-height third floor above the cornice. But, due to the retention of the pediments, the elevation appears compromised and rather top-heavy.

16 Norfolk Crescent Built in 1798, Norfolk Crescent is attributed to John Palmer. But John Pinch's known involvement in the works, and the similarity of the elevation to his later buildings, suggest that he could be the author.
In the foreground is the nightwatchman's hut of 1793: could this be an early interpretation of the Choragic Monument of Lysicrates [50]?

and the building continues grandly up to a second, less pronounced cornice and parapet. The introduction of a fourth storey with rooms free of the encumbrances of roof hips and valleys is understandable in economic terms. Northumberland Buildings was a speculative venture on Baldwin's part and clearly he saw that such extra accommodation would give considerable value and saleability to his building. But the use of an attic storey in Bath architecture was actually something which predated Palladianism: it can be seen in Marshal Wade's house in the Abbey Churchyard, built in 1715. Visually, Northumberland Buildings is slightly awkward and the attic storey reads rather like a later extension. Had the original small, square shape of the windows been retained throughout, it probably would have expressed the weighty solidity such a storey requires.

The four storey façade was next seen at Norfolk Crescent [16]. Walter Ison suggests that the architect of this scheme, started in 1798, was probably John Palmer, and that John Pinch was called in to complete the joinery and ironwork – for here there are lampholders of identical design to those at New Sydney Place. But, considering Pinch's five later terraces, Norfolk Crescent could be more his.

The major difference between Norfolk Crescent and the earlier Northumberland Buildings is that the pediment has become detached from the entablature and now is presented above the attic storey, while below the entablature Giant Order pilasters are reintroduced. This was the arrangement which Pinch adopted for his five major terraces in Bath, although only in New Sydney Place and Sion Hill Place does he employ a pediment. When compared, these terraces can be seen to have a number of common elements which make up their four storey elevation [17]. From the top they are all finished with a parapet above the upper cornice and, in the attic storey, they all have a square or nearly square window, resting firmly within the middle of that storey. Each building then employs a heavy entablature, in all cases plain, except for Sion Hill Place, where the Pompeian scroll is introduced. The longer, second floor mezzanine windows at New Sydney Place and Sion Hill Place are now linked by a sill band while in the others they still remain free floating; and where no string courses divide the mezzanine storey from the *piano nobile* below, hoods are introduced over the *piano nobile* windows to suggest the break. In one instance, at Cavendish Place, both window hoods and string course are used. In all cases the *piano nobile* windows are long and

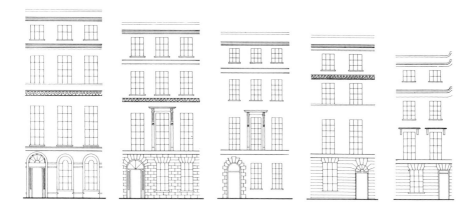

17 Elevations by John Pinch   Pinch's five elevations – New Sydney Place, Cavendish Place, Cavendish Crescent, Sion Hill Place and Raby Place – are all variations on the same theme.

thin, running right down to the *piano rustica*. Here the greatest variety is found, for no two terraces are exactly the same. In three cases rustication is used to emphasise the base of the building: chamfered rustication at Cavendish Place and in two later instances, Sion Hill Place and Raby Place, banded rustication. A further suggestion of the solidity of the *piano rustica* is provided by the use of rusticated, round-headed door openings in three of the terraces, Cavendish Place, Cavendish Crescent and Sion Hill Place. New Sydney Place has plain, round-headed door and window openings as well.

This brief comment on the composition of the elevations should be complemented by some remarks on the details employed. The most noticeable decorative element is the Pompeian or Vitruvian scroll, also known more descriptively as a wave scroll, and sometimes, a running dog. It was a decorative feature common to both the Palladians and to the Adam generation which followed. The arch-Palladians, William Kent and Lord Burlington, had used it in the Egyptian Hall at Holkham, Norfolk (c1735), and it can be found in the pages of Sir William Chambers' *Treatise on Civil Architecture* (1759) as a Palladian decorative element, where it is described as an 'ornament for flat members'. Chambers himself used it internally at Melbourne House, Piccadilly (1771) and previously had intended it for the Temple of Peace at Kew (1763, unfinished). But it would be wrong to consider its use in Bath as a Palladian feature.

The rejection of Palladianism and the search for, and expression of, new sources of Classicism – Neo-Classicism – had started in about 1760. This was the generation of Robert and James Adam and, as shall be shown, James Stuart and Nicholas Revett. It is in this context that this decorative element is best referred to as the Pompeian scroll: Pompeii, a new source of Classical reference, was first excavated in 1748 and from then on became a major stage on the Grand Tour. Robert Adam had visited Herculaneum in 1755 and his brother James inspected Pompeii in 1761. Ten years later, in the remodelling of Kenwood House in Hampstead, Robert Adam made lavish use, externally, of the Pompeian scroll. Elevations and decorative details from Kenwood were published in 1774, in part two of the first volume of *The Works in Architecture of Robert and James Adam* [18], and it is clearly these, rather than Chambers' examples, which provide the provenance of Pinch's terraces. The most telling illustration is the elevation of the south or garden front [19], where not only does the Pompeian scroll appear in the 'string which separates the attic from the bed chamber storey', as at Sion Hill Place, but the whole arrangement of the façade, with the exception of the pilasters, is that of Pinch's four storey façades. The only point of reinterpretation on Pinch's part is the substitution of windows for the decorative panels in the mezzanine storey. Not even Baldwin's Northumberland Buildings, where the Pompeian scroll appears, are so clearly derivative.

The window hoods which appear at New Sydney Place, Cavendish Place, Cavendish Crescent and Raby Place represent an

18 Pompeian or Vitruvian scrollwork Decorative scrollwork, used by Robert Adam at Kenwood House and illustrated in *The Works in Architecture of Robert and James Adam*, was employed by John Pinch at New Sydney Place, Cavendish Place and Sion Hill Place.

old theme stylised in the Neo-Classical manner. Canopies, cornices supported on consoles, such as Pinch was to use, had been common since James Gibbs published his influential *Book on Architecture* in 1728, and variations along this theme were published in a number of copy-books throughout the eighteenth century. Notable amongst these, and heavily influenced by Gibbs, was Batty Langley's *City and County Builder's and Workman's Treasury of Designs* (1739). By the time William Pain published *The Practical House Carpenter* in 1805, fashion, not a little inspired by the Adams, had drawn out the consoles to a length of some 20 to 24 inches and this is reflected in the designs offered, some of which, incidentally, had been published as early as 1789. Such forms Pinch employs, and in some cases, demonstrates the continuing influence of the Adams by adding, with the fascia, a festoon.

Pinch's architecture in these five terraces was not wholly derivative. He is clearly influenced by the Adams and also the continuing Palladian tradition of late eighteenth-century Bath. But in his use of an astylar architecture, façades without either columns or pilasters, he takes the lead from Baldwin and boldly turns the corner into the nineteenth century.

Baldwin was greatly influential for Pinch. Common to both their

19 Kenwood House, Hampstead, London   The elevation of Kenwood House, published in *The Works in Architecture of Robert and James Adam*, provides a possible precedent for John Pinch's Sion Hill Place and his treatment of four storey façades generally.

work are the four storey façades, Pompeian scrolls and delicately decorated window hoods. Since Pinch took over from Baldwin as surveyor to the Darlington Estates, it is not unlikely that Baldwin had some influence over Pinch's early work there: indeed, Pinch was endorsing drawings on leases for Henrietta Street and part of Great Pulteney Street as early as 1797. Furthermore, New Sydney Place follows the plan of buildings Baldwin had intended to lay out around Sydney Gardens. Had Baldwin maintained his position as surveyor to the Darlington Estates, it is unlikely that the architectural development of the early nineteenth-century terraces of Bath would have been very different.

20 Sir Joshua Reynolds, *Mrs Peter Beckford*   Sir Joshua Reynold's Neo-
Classical portrait of 1782, which used to hang in William Beckford's house at 20
Lansdown Crescent, shows Beckford's cousin's wife sacrificing to Hygeia, the
Goddess of Health.

CHAPTER 3

Neo-Classical Architecture

NEO-CLASSICISM

The influence of Neo-Classicism, in Robert and James Adam's Roman manner, had now been introduced. Theirs was not an unrepentant, hard-line adhesion to the forms of antiquity; as speculators as well as designers they saw the necessity of recognising the established affection for Palladianism, and thus its influence can be seen clearly in their buildings. Yet even so, their greatest speculation, the Adelphi in London, was virtually their ruin.

Neo-Classicism affected all aspects of the visual arts. From the late eighteenth century visitors to Bath would have been familiar with the high waist-lines and ballooning sleeves of the ladies' dresses, the tight curls of their hair, and the elegant swags and drapes of the furnishings. These were the images of the great French painter Jacques-Louis David and the Empire of Napoleon. In England, the influence of Neo-Classicism was seen first in the works of painters such as Johann Zoffany (1734–1810) and Angelica Kauffman (1741–1807). It was, however, the paintings of Sir Joshua Reynolds (1723–1792) which dominated portraiture for much of the eighteenth century. There used to hang, in William Beckford's house at Lansdown Crescent, Reynold's portrait of his cousin's wife, Mrs Peter Beckford [20], first exhibited in 1782. The portrait is intensely Classical both in its composition and its allusion. This description of Mrs Peter Beckford was written in 1838:

She is represented approaching an altar partially obscured by clouds of incense that she may sacrifice to Hygeia, and turning round looking at the spectator. The background is quite Titianesque; it is composed of sky and the columns of the temple, the light breaking on the pillars in that forcible manner you see on the stems of trees in some of Titian's backgrounds. The colouring of the picture is in fine preservation, a delicate lilac scarf floats over the dress, the figure is grace and elegance itself, and the drawing perfect; the general effect is brilliancy, richness, and astonishing softness. 'Sir Joshua took the greatest pleasure and delight in painting that picture, [said William Beckford] as it was left entirely to his own refined taste. The lady was in ill-health at the time it was done, and Sir Joshua most charmingly conceived the idea of a sacrifice to the Goddess of Health. Vain hope! Her disorder was fatal.'

The best introduction to the architecture of the ancient world was the great folio volumes published by the early travellers to southern Italy and the Levant – Dalmatia, Greece, and coastal Turkey. The first such folios of resounding significance appeared in the 1760s. Robert Adam's *Ruins of the Palace of the Emperor Diocletian at Spalatro*, published in 1764, demonstrated quite clearly that the Palladians were not the final authority on Roman architecture. The greatest impact of the Adam revolution, despite the examples we have been considering, was in interior design. Here the simple, rectangular rooms of the Palladian's domestic architecture were replaced by series of imaginatively arranged, elegantly decorated rooms, unified down to the details of the door furniture by a sophisticated decorative scheme that subtly blended Roman and Renaissance motifs. Consider, for instance, Kedleston Hall in Derbyshire (1760–1770) or Syon House in Middlesex (1762–1769). The success of this harmonious blend was so lasting that Adamesque decorative features are still readily available today.

THE GREEK REVIVAL

In 1762, two years before Robert Adam published his folio on *Spalatro*, another Scot, James Stuart, with an Englishman, Nicholas Revett, published the first volume of their monumental work on *The Antiquities of Athens*. These volumes represented the first accurate survey of Greek classical remains and were to serve as the primary source books for the Greek Revival in Britain. Yet, unlike Robert Adam's book, the immediate effect was limited. James Stuart and a few other Levantines introduced Greek features into their work, but it was not until some forty years later that the effect of *The Antiquities of Athens* became apparent: for the Greek Revival was a phenomenon of the early nineteenth century.

Whereas the first volume of *The Antiquities of Athens* was concerned largely with the decoration of buildings, the second volume, which appeared in 1789, turned its attention to the glories of the Acropolis. Although Stuart had long since bought out Revett's interest in the venture, it was his own indolence which delayed for twenty-six years the publication of the second volume. This, and his own inability to capitalize upon his opportunities, are largely the reasons that the effect of *The Antiquities of Athens* was so long delayed. It was the fault more of the man than of the style.

Throughout the second half of the eighteenth century the new interest in classical Greece had been nurtured and controlled by a group of wealthy patrons known as the Society of Dilettanti. Their interest was in the accurate, archaeological recordings of the ancient remains. Political events in Europe helped further their interests. The Revolutionary and Napoleonic Wars made it impossible for the young British gentleman on the Grand Tour to visit France and much of Italy, so he turned his attention to the east, to the Levant. Since the British navy dominated the Mediterranean this presented no particular problem: in Greece folk-hero status was accorded to Admiral Lord Nelson and, slightly later, to Lord Byron. The number of books that were to follow Adam and Stuart and Revett's seminal works was prodigious. G M Dumont and T Major published independently on the Greek remains near Naples, at Paestum (1764 and 1768); Nicholas Revett wrote, without Stuart, on *Ionian Antiquities* (1769 and 1797); William Wilkins recorded his tours in *Magna Graecia* (1807); and W H Inwood published *Fragments of Athenian Architecture* (1827). Yet despite these and other (notably French) publications, Stuart and Revett's *Antiquities of Athens* dominated the field. This was largely because they were British, and because of James Stuart's own reputation as an architect: he had been dubbed 'Athenian' Stuart by Sir John Soane. Furthermore, their volumes continued to be published over a prolonged period:

Volume 2 appeared in 1789 and three others followed in 1794, 1816 and 1830. The last two volumes, being posthumous, were largely edited by C R Cockerell, himself a Greek scholar, as is clearly shown in his Bank of England branch bank in Bristol (1844).

The greatest expression of Greek Revival architecture in Bath was by a local architect, H E Goodridge, and it is clear that his main source of reference was *The Antiquities of Athens*, although his work was not to appear until the mid-1820s. It took a number of visiting architects working in the first quarter of the nineteenth century to introduce Greek Revival architecture to Bath, and to effect successfully the transition from Palladio and Adam's Roman Classicism to Greek.

This transition was first worked in a public building, the Theatre Royal, in 1804–5, by the London architect George Dance. The younger Dance, aged 63, knew Bath well and had good contacts. He had visited the city in 1766 or 1767, soon after work on the Royal Crescent had begun, and had returned to London to create his own crescent and circus in the Minories at Tower Hill in 1768. This was to be the first use of these forms in London. At Bath he knew Charles Pratt, then first Baron Camden and in 1766, the new Lord Chancellor. Camden had been Recorder of Bath since 1759 and was later to receive the freedom of the city. His arms, which include three elephant heads *erased argent*, appear in the tympanum of the pediments at Camden Crescent and Camden Terrace, each bearing his name, and elephants appear again over the doorways. Dance's introduction to Camden had been made through his brother-in-law and his cousin, who, like Camden, were involved in the East India Company. His friendship with Camden remained lifelong – there are copies of portraits of Camden drawn by George Dance (1793) and by his brother Nathaniel, at the British Museum and the National Portrait Gallery respectively – and it was for Camden that Dance laid out the estate in north London which bears his name today.

At Bath, Dance had another close friend, John Palmer (1742–1818). It was he who set up the first mail coach between Bath and London with the support of Camden, who in 1782 had put the idea before William Pitt, then Chancellor of the Exchequer. Four years later, Palmer was to make a second marriage to a Miss Pratt, probably one of Camden's relations.

By the beginning of the nineteenth century John Palmer was at the height of his power in Bath. He was mayor of the city in 1796 and 1808, and had sat at Westminster in 1801, 1802, 1806 and 1807, before accepting the Chiltern Hundreds in 1808 and passing the seat on to his son. He was also wealthy, receiving a pension of £3,000 a year from 1793 and eventually, in 1813, a payment of £50,000 for his services as comtroller-general of the post office.

In 1776 Palmer had taken over the running of the Theatre Royal, which had been established by letters patent issued to his father in 1768, and in 1779 he became lessee of the theatre at Bristol. But by 1804 the Theatre Royal on Beauford Square was quite inadequate and in need of modernisation. In August that year a subscription was opened to cover the building cost, and preparation for building began. As yet there was no design, but that November George Dance visited Bath to take the waters. The resulting commission produced some fifteen sheets of alternative elevation and interior designs which are now held at Sir John Soane's Museum. In this context, it is important to separate John Palmer of the Theatre Royal from John Palmer, the City Architect and designer of Lansdown Crescent, whose dates, c1738–1817, are confusingly close. It is unlikely that the owner of the Theatre Royal would have commissioned designs from a London friend and architect, only to pass them on to the City Architect for building. The foundation stone for the theatre had been laid as early as December 1804, before Dance's designs were complete and, therefore, before they could have been passed on to the City Architect. Thus it appears possible that the common attribution of this building to the City Architect is a confusion resulting from the similarity of names.

The designs George Dance produced owed something to the Palladian tradition, but also clearly showed the influence of the Greek Revival and internally, more exotic eastern architecture. At the Theatre Royal, the flat treatment of the façade, the stylised pilasters and the refined Classicism of the roofline represent an almost abstract architecture, very close to that which his former pupil, Sir John Soane, was developing so effectively at this time.

In the alternative designs for the Beauford Square façade [21] it is the decorative details which change. Pilasters are introduced and then removed, and Greek acroteria, pediments and lyres are all tried out above the blocking course [22]. Yet, throughout, the frieze remains the same: theatrical masks linked by festoons, and the Royal crest is always displayed over the centre. The final design [23], with pilasters and four carved stone lyres, is less Hellenic in its references than a literal translation of something from *The Antiquities of Athens* might have been. The abstract

21 The Theatre Royal, preliminary design

22 The Theatre Royal, preliminary pediment design
[21–22] Pediments, acroteria and statuary were introduced and then removed
from these preliminary designs for the Theatre Royal by George Dance, but the
royal crest was allowed to remain.

23 The Theatre Royal, elevation   At the Theatre Royal in 1804–05, George
Dance provided the first noticeable departure from Palladianism in a major
public building in Bath.

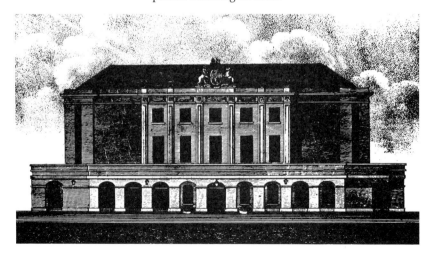

NEO-CLASSICAL ARCHITECTURE

quality of much of the architecture is far removed from the Palladian source which the overall composition suggests, and the inclusion of lyres, the ancient instrument used by the Greeks for the accompaniment of poetry, provides a suitably theatrical allusion.

It was Sir John Soane's protegé, the extraordinarily talented but hopelessly unreliable Joseph Michael Gandy, who built the most uncompromisingly Greek Revival building Bath was to see. Despite an auspicious start to his career, he achieved little more than being a draughtsman to Sir John Soane, to whom he was to be indebted for financial aid for most of his life. Yet Soane, who was not a talented draughtsman, needed Gandy as much as Gandy needed Soane. Without Gandy's extraordinary skill the representation of Soane's designs would have never been quite so unforgettable.

Following a Grand Tour, curtailed by the unsettled state of Europe, Gandy had worked in practice on his own from 1801. In 1803 he exhibited the design for a house with a gallery on Sion Hill for the painter Thomas Barker at the Royal Academy. It was a modified version of this design which was built, probably being completed by 1805, for in that year an exhibition was advertised 'in the new picture gallery on Sion Hill'. Strangely, it was not until 1818 that Gandy exhibited the built house at the Royal Academy.

The early design for the building known as Doric House [24] formed the basis on which the second design was worked. The common element was the treatment of the long ground floor façade facing onto Sion Hill. This consisted of a *tetrastyle-in-antis* Doric elevation; that is a five bay façade of four columns contained within two *antae* or terminating pilasters, all set on a hefty plinth. In the first scheme [25] this was finished with a simplified Doric entablature, *sans* metopes and triglyphs, and a blocking course hiding rooflights behind. In this instance the columns were fluted and a sculptured frieze decorated the upper part of the wall behind.

In the final scheme [26] the fluting and frieze have both gone and a second storey, now of a smaller Doric Order with windows, has been added above the entablature of the first, which sports a boldly projecting modillion cornice. The line of the corners and columns is carried through to the skyline in the form of stylised acroterion, much as Soane might have used. These appear again on the pediment above the pilastered end elevation to the south.

In both schemes the arrangement of Doric columns *in antis*,

24 Doric House Joseph Michael Gandy built Doric House as a picture gallery for Thomas Barker between 1803 and 1805.

25 Doric House, preliminary design Joseph Michael Gandy's first design for Doric House, exhibited at the Royal Academy in 1803, was derived, in elevation, from the Temple of Zeus Olympus at Agrigentum, Sicily.

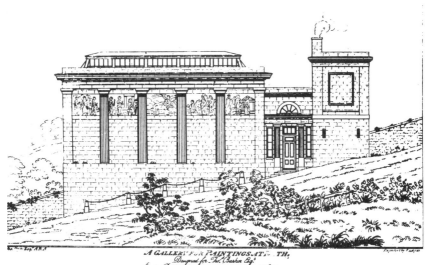

A GALLERY FOR PAINTINGS AT ... TH.

against a blind wall, is typical of the side elevations of early Doric temples in southern Italy and Sicily. In the Temple of Zeus Olympus at Agrigentum in Sicily engaged half columns flank the *naos* or inner chamber in the manner of Gandy's first design. Although not contained between *antae*, the side wall at Zeus Olympus is divided into a blank lower half and, above a string course, a windowed upper half which Gandy has reinterpreted as a frieze. By the employment of a double tier of Doric columns in the final scheme, Gandy makes immediate reference to the Temple of Poseidon [27] at Paestum, near Naples in Italy, where the inner walls of the *naos* are flanked by Doric columns of just such an arrangement. Now in its ruinous stage, these formerly interior columns at Paestum are exposed to the sky, thus suggesting fresh interpretation.

Gandy's use of the Doric Order in Bath is simple in the extreme, despite the quirks of the concave capitals and the rebate at the base. By employing unfluted columns Gandy was trying something relatively rare in English architecture. The greatest exponent, hitherto, of this simple or primitive form was Soane although others, including John Nash and James Wyatt, tried it once or twice. By the time Gandy built Doric House, there were only about a dozen examples of the unfluted Doric in the country.

The house is quite original within his own small *ouvre*, although some of the fittings can be seen elsewhere. Soon after he exhibited the first design for Doric House, Gandy built offices for the Phoenix Fire and Pelican Life Insurance Companies in London. Although this building displayed a more standard fluted Doric Order the fireplaces, now at the Geffrye Museum in London, were of the same Egyptian caryatid theme which Gandy was to use at Doric House. Shortly after Doric House was completed Gandy was called to remodel Storr's Hall at Windermere and here, in another Greek essay, he used an elliptical rooflight above the hall as he had done at Doric House.

Doric House, as first designed and as later executed, is important. The first design, exhibited at the Royal Academy, must have been recognised by the academicians for its quality for, despite having done little independent work, Gandy was elected an Associate of the Royal Academy in 1803. Surprisingly his client Thomas Barker had, by comparison, little involvement with the Royal Academy and his name appears but occasionally in their catalogues. Yet he was an artist of considerable reputation and needed to entertain in a generous manner which would not

26 Doric House

27 The Temple of Poseidon, Paestum   The final version of Joseph Michael Gandy's design for Doric House, completed by 1805, took its elevation from the naos of the Temple of Poseidon at Paestum, Italy.

compromise his artistic sensibilities. Doric House provided him with just this opportunity. It was right up to date stylistically and carefully planned on an awkward site. It was both a house and, as the bland walls demonstrate, a gallery. When, in 1825, he painted on the inner face of these walls the great Classical fresco of *The Massacre of the Greeks on the Island of Scios* the concept became complete.

It was a younger architect, but no less a Classical scholar, whom the proprietors of Bath's Lower Assembly Rooms engaged in 1808 to remodel their failing institution. William Wilkins, whose name is now best known as the architect of the National Gallery in London, was but thirty years old and in practice in Cambridge, where he was a Fellow of Gonville and Caius. He had travelled extensively in Italy and the Levant between 1801 and 1804, and in 1807 published drawings made while abroad in *The Antiquities of Magna Graecia*. Coincident with this publication he secured in

28 Destruction of the Kingston Assembly Rooms, Bath The destruction of the Kingston or Lower Assembly Rooms by fire in 1820 destroyed any interior work which William Wilkins might have done in 1808–09. Nevertheless, his massive portico did survive.

29 The Lower Assembly Rooms

1806 the commission for the new Downing College at Cambridge. This scheme had attracted some publicity; in 1804 Thomas Hope had written his *Observations on the Plans and Elevations . . . for Downing College*, calling for a design in the Neo-Greek and significantly referring to Wilkins as a contender; the next year Wilkins had actually exhibited, at the Royal Academy, Neo-Greek designs for the south and entrance fronts. And when the College committee came to make their decision in 1806 they had already consulted George Dance, whose designs for the Theatre Royal in Bath were then under construction.

Not knowing who the proprietors of the Lower Assembly Rooms were at this time, it is difficult to be sure why Wilkins received this contract so far from home.* One can speculate that Dance might well have made a recommendation for Wilkins: but then Wilkins was already beginning to make a name for himself.

Wilkins' proposals for the Lower Assembly Rooms consisted of the addition of a large, hexastyle Doric portico, and presumably, some work to the interior. But the building was burned out on 21 December, 1820 [28], and no record of any interior work has come

* Writing in 'A Trial-Run for Regent's Park: Repton and Nash at Bath, 1796' (*Bath History*, vol III, 1990)' Tim Mowl states that Wilkins' father, William Wilkins (1751–1815), had provided, between 1802 and 1804, a scheme for 175 houses set around a square on the Ham where St John the Divine now stands. Commissioned by Lord Newark, it was not built.

30 The Grange, Hampshire

to light. Yet Wilkins' work was extensive enough to provide material for the Royal Academy in both 1808 and 1809.

The portico he added is very significant, both in the development of his own work and as part of the Greek Revival in Britain. If the argument of dates as presented by R W Liscombe in

31 The Temple of Concord, Agrigentum, Sicily
[29–31] William Wilkins added the hexastyle, Doric portico to the Lower Assembly Rooms in 1808–09, at just the time he was building The Grange near Northington, Hampshire. Both designs are based upon the Temple of Concord at Agrigentum, Sicily, which he had illustrated in *Magna Graecia* in 1807.

William Wilkins is accepted, and there seems to be no reason why it should not be, then the designs for the Doric portico at the Lower Assembly Rooms [29] precedes that similar and more celebrated portico he built contemporaneously at The Grange, near Northington, Hampshire (1809) [30]. The fact that the work at The Grange was completed some months before the Lower Assembly Rooms reopened on 1 November 1810 is possibly because it was of brick and stucco and could be erected more quickly than even the Bath masons could work stone for the Lower Assembly Rooms.

The Grange is extremely important: Pevsner said of it, 'this was one of the first determined *credos* in the coming Grecian mode, highly exciting and far from domestic.' Wilkins brought, for the first time, the massive scale of fifth-century BC Doric of Parthenon proportions to English parkland. This was a very determined attempt, as Liscombe comments, to 'out-Pericles' what George Dance had done, but only in tetrastyle, at neighbouring Stratton Park six years earlier.

The Lower Assembly Rooms must be equally important. Public rooms deserved a powerful, public style, and the grand proportions of Wilkins' portico did just that. Wilkins could have derived the design from a number of sources he had seen on his European tour. The most likely model would be the fifth-century BC Temple of Concord at Agrigentum [31] in Sicily, or possibly the Temple of Juno Lucina, at the same site. Both are recorded in *Magna Graecia*. Wilkins had also visited mainland Greece – his *Atheniensia* was written in 1816 as the 'result of observations made during a residency there in the year 1802' – and the Theseion in Athens provides another model for the Lower Assembly Rooms.

The fire of 1820 necessitated extensive rebuilding of the Lower Assembly Rooms [32]. This work was done by George Allen Underwood, who was at this time (1822–3) surveyor to the County of Somerset. Underwood had worked for Sir John Soane between 1807 and 1815 and would have been well versed in Greek architecture. Indeed the interiors, when rebuilt, were quite Soanesque. His work to the exterior of the building displays much confidence: he retained Wilkins' portico and added a heavy and rather dominating attic storey. And if contemporary prints can be read clearly, it would appear to be he rather than Wilkins who built the small, *in antis*, Doric portico at the side [33], a feature which he might well have picked up from Wilkins himself, who added just such a portico to Kingweston House, near Glastonbury in Somerset, at about this time. Regrettably, the Lower Assembly

Rooms were demolished in 1933. Until recently, its awkward triangular site overlooking Parade Gardens was known, eponymously, as 'Bog Island.'

Wilkins next returned to Bath to build in 1817. This time the building remains, the Friends' Meeting House in York Street, which he designed as a Hall for the Freemasons. A brass plate laid in the foundations of the Hall referring to 'Brother Wilkins, Architect' would also indicate his affiliation to the fraternity. And here one might speculate that the buildings directly opposite the Hall are also by Wilkins. Nos. 11 to 15 York Street [34] not only reflect the details of the Hall in the capitals and entablature, but also present a pediment to reflect, directly, that of the Hall. But no documentation as to their authorship has come to light.

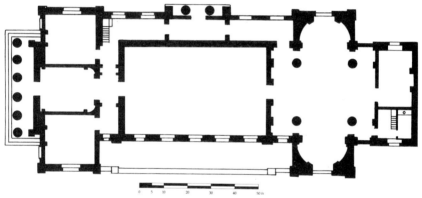

32 The Lower Assembly Rooms, plan

33 The Lower Assembly Rooms
[32–33] Following the fire of 1820, the Lower Assembly Rooms were rebuilt by George Allen Underwood in 1822–23 and remained, as the Royal Science and Literary Institution, until demolition in 1932 vacated the site for 'Bog Island'. In the rebuilding, Underwood retained William Wilkins' portico and, so it would appear, added an entrance portico on the west side, opening onto The Walks.

There is, however, a drawing retained at Columbia University, New York, that is thought by Liscombe to be a preliminary design for the Hall. It shows an Ionic tetrastyle portico flanked by three window bays, *in antis*. Liscombe bases his argument on the presence of three statues, in niches, which he identifies as the Masonic symbols of Faith, Hope and Charity. Indeed, these statues did feature in the Hall when eventually built. Yet elsewhere in this drawing, the iconography of the building is quite wrong. The central door is open and beckoning and the windows afford no privacy: the blank doorway, blind windows and rooflights which, in the realised design, ensured Masonic privacy, are much more the iconography one would expect. It seems more likely that this design was for another client.

The Freemasons' Hall in York Street [35] is faced with a large Ionic portico, *distyle-in-antis*, flanked by (originally blind) Ionic windows, the whole set up on a plinth or stylobate. The building

34 11–15 York Street   These buildings in York Street so closely resemble the Freemasons' Hall opposite, that it is hard to believe that they are not also by the same architect, William Wilkins.

35 The Freemasons' Hall, York Street, elevation

36 The Freemasons' Hall, York Street, plan

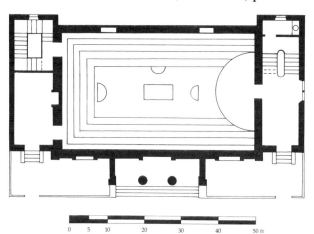

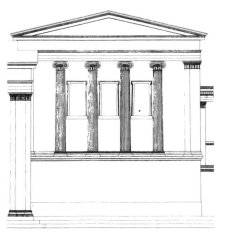

37 The Erectheion, Athens, elevation

[35–37] William Wilkin's Freemasons' Hall of 1817 originally had blind windows and was surmounted by statues of Faith, Hope and Charity. The *tetrastyle-in-antis* portico, derived from the west front of the Erectheion in Athens, was similarly blind, and access to the top-lit building was achieved through the rusticated, arched doorways at either side.

lends little to the otherwise domestic scale on that side of the street, but Wilkins cleverly knits the two together. The portico, in fact, does not provide an entrance to the building [36]: this is by way of rusticated arched openings in each of the small side wings, free of the stylobate, more domestic in scale and almost Palladian in appearance.

The Ionic treatment of the exterior probably owes a lot to the Erectheion in Athens [37]. There the west elevation has an Ionic portico, *tetrastyle-in-antis*. Wilkins had illustrated this in his *Atheniensia* and again later in his *Prolusiones Architectonicae* (1837). Yet the Freemasons' Hall is different: it is Ionic, but *distyle-in-antis*. Wilkins' travels around the Mediterranean had taken him to Asia Minor and there he might have seen the rock-cut tombs of Lycia, in southern Turkey, just across the sea from Rhodes. Two of these early tombs, now in the British Museum, illustrate the rare use of an Ionic *distyle-in-antis* portico.

The growing interest in Greek Revival and the tenacious survival of the Palladian tradition is demonstrated well in Bath by a curious and not particularly attractive church located at the beginning of the London Road – the Walcot Chapel [38]. Completed in 1815, it falls in between Wilkins' two visits to Bath. Whereas the main façade is of a rather thin Palladian style – pilasters along the *piano nobile* and rusticated stones in the *piano rustica* – the porch is uncompromisingly Greek Doric. That this is all surface treatment, and the foibles of fashion, becomes apparent when the building is compared to the Lambeth Chapel in Lambeth Road, London, built about 1817 [39]. Both chapels were designed and built by the Rev William Jenkins, and are apparently the same basic building, but the surface treatment of the latter is now attuned to the round arches and slender porches of the speculative terraces of Regency London.

Wilkins' role in turning the Greek Revival from a garden conceit to an architectural expression of power and dignity was considerable. His Greek designs, winning over Roman schemes in the competitions for Downing College, Cambridge and in the next year the East India College at Haileybury, Hertfordshire, served also to establish an acceptable style for collegiate or institutional architecture. The impetus was maintained for many years – Downing College was not completed until 1820 – and in 1827–8 Wilkins was adapting temples of a scale as vast as that of Apollo at Didyma, near Miletus in Caria, to the new University College buildings in London.

38 Walcot Chapel, London Road

39 Lambeth Chapel, Lambeth Road, London

[38–39] Architectural style, whether Palladian, Greek or Regency, is little more than skin deep in the Walcot and Lambeth chapels, built in 1815 and c1817 by the Rev. William Jenkins, an itinerant Wesleyan minister with an architectural training.

It was two London architects, Samuel and Philip Flood Page, who designed the most striking collegiate example of Greek Revival architecture in the west country, Partis College [40]. Built in 1825–7 to provide a home for thirty 'decayed gentlewomen', its

40 Partis College

41 Downing College, Cambridge

42 The Erectheion, Athens, elevation

43 Partis College
[40–43] Samuel and Philip Flood Page's elevation for Partis College, built in 1825–27, was probably derived from William Wilkin's work of 1806 at Downing College, Cambridge which, in its turn, was derived from the east front of the Erectheion at Athens. There is also, in the heavy blocking courses on the end pavilions, a suggestion of the influence of Sir John Soane. See [68].

open-sided quadrangular form and Ionic portico owe more than a little to Downing College, Cambridge [41]. The hexastyle portico at Downing College was, in turn, derived from the east elevation of the Erectheion in Athens [42]. This, once again, had been discussed in Wilkins' own *Atheniensia* and was illustrated in the second volume of Stuart and Revett's *Antiquities of Athens*. The long ranges of rooms at Partis College [43] terminating in pavilions, pilastered but now with heavy blocking courses in place of pediments, once again emulate Downing College. Here, too, there might be a little of Sir John Soane's influence: Philip Flood Page had trained under Joseph Henry Good, a pupil of Soane. It is surprising that such a striking but admittedly derivative work as Partis College was never followed up. Samuel Flood Page designed a Gothic church in Middlesex, but subsequently took orders and went into the priesthood: of his younger brother no more is known.

Meanwhile, Wilkins' one surviving building in Bath, the Freemasons' Hall, proved to be the inspiration for the first major job undertaken by a young man who was to become the most significant Bath-based architect of the nineteenth century. His name was Henry Edmund Goodridge.

Born in Bath in 1797 to James Goodridge, a successful local builder and later agent to the Darlington Estate until 1835, he

44 The Argyle Chapel, Laura Place, elevation   Built by H E Goodridge in 1821, the Argyle Chapel clearly draws upon William Wilkins' Freemasons' Hall completed four years earlier.

served his apprenticeship under John Lowder, probably at the time when Lowder became surveyor to the city of Bath (1817–23). His first real commission on setting up in practice involved work on St Thomas à Becket, Widcombe – probably the doorway to the crypt at street level – in 1820. The rebuilding of the Argyle Chapel in 1821 came next.

The Argyle Chapel [44] in Laura Place was originally built to a design of Thomas Baldwin in 1789. The remarkable oratory skills of the Rev. William Jay must have proved popular amongst his Nonconformist congregation, for in 1804 the Chapel needed enlargement, and by 1821 it had to be enlarged again. It is possible that Goodridge received the commission through his friendship with Matilda Yockney, the daughter of a member of the Chapel's Improvement Committee, whom he married the following year. It is also possible that it came from the minister directly, for Jay was the son of a stonecutter and mason from Timsbury and had served an apprenticeship in this trade: he had, in fact, worked with his father on the building of Fonthill Abbey for William Beckford, and Beckford was soon to be Goodridge's patron.

Goodridge's design for the new façade at the Argyle Chapel owes a lot to Wilkins' Freemasons' Hall. Like the earlier building, the Argyle Chapel displays an Ionic portico, *distyle-in-antis*, protecting not a blind doorway but a large window. On either side, between terminal pilasters, there are Greek Ionic doorways, placed where Wilkins had put his blind windows. Charles Robert Cockerell, who visited Bath in January 1823, was not impressed by Goodridge's façade – 'apparently an entrance to a church tho' not having properly that character.' His comments would have been equally applicable to Wilkins' earlier building in York Street. '. . . whatever the Building is there is gross impropriety in having the entrances at the sides. They should have been only under logge in Portico, whereas in back of Portico is a window purched as a surbase. The side doors should have been windows.' Where the Argyle Chapel really differs from the Freemasons' Hall is in the addition of an attic. storey, above the main entablature, which is then crowned by the pediment. This treatment is rather unusual – perhaps just the early effort of a young man – but it does offer a reminder of Pinch's Sion Hill Place, then just completing. Sadly, the upper part of this façade was insensitively altered forty years later by the Bath architects Hickes and Isaac.

Goodridge's next major work, following on from the Argyle Chapel, was the most significant of his career: in terms of architectural history, it is the most important work he did. This was the Lansdown Tower, built for William Beckford in 1825–6. Exactly how Goodridge came by this commission is a mystery. Possibly some form of introduction had been made by the Rev William Jay, but that would seem unlikely. Goodridge had made a watercolour drawing of Beckford's Fonthill Abbey in 1817 – it survives in the Victoria Art Gallery in Bath – so maybe he had known Beckford from that date. In any event, when Beckford moved to Bath in 1822 he immediately needed the services of an architect.

In that year Beckford bought 20 Lansdown Crescent from Sir Walter James and soon after the adjacent house across the mews, 1 Lansdown Place West, then called West Wing. These he linked with a bridge at first floor level [7] and it would seem likely that even at this early date Goodridge was his architect, for details both of the bridge and of a pedimented and arched doorway thrust

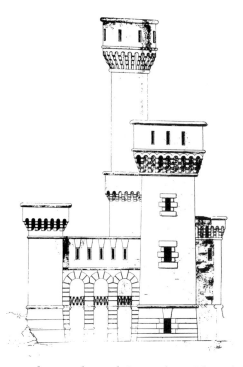

45 The Lansdown Tower, 'Saxon' design, elevation This early design for the Lansdown Tower, prepared by H E Goodridge in 1823, demonstrates the massing and articulation which he was to use in the final design.

underneath and into the side of Lansdown Place West reflect Goodridge's later work.

It would seem that Beckford, irascible and not a little eccentric, sought a young architect who would be more amenable to his wishes than one might suspect his architect at Fonthill Abbey, the middle-aged James Wyatt, to have been. Clearly Beckford found Goodridge to his liking. Goodridge was later to write of his patron: 'His paroxysms of passion when I first knew him were most fearful; but in his later years he obtained a wonderful mastery over himself, and which was seldom broken through. He used to say that he could not now afford it.'

In 1823 Beckford purchased some land with good views at the top of Lansdown, near the turnpike road, and soon Goodridge had drawn up a number of designs for a tower. Ison tells us of one resembling a Gothic lighthouse; another, according to a report in *The Observer* of October 1823, was a 'Saxon tower'. A drawing for something of this sort has survived [45]. But the final design displays a Picturesque fusion of archaeological Greek Revival and the more relaxed Tuscan villa style of the Italian *campagna* [46]. The Tuscan villa style, which is discussed in chapter four, was reserved for the two and three storey buildings at the base of the tower [47]. The tower itself, after rising sheer and devoid of decoration for

46 The Lansdown Tower

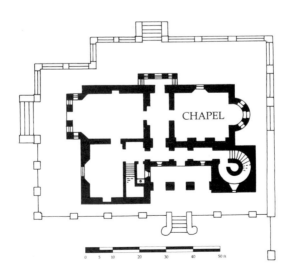

47 The Lansdown Tower, plan

[46–47] In the final design of 1824 for the Lansdown Tower, H E Goodridge combines Greek detail with Tuscan massing in a fusion of Picturesque charm.

about 90 feet, suddenly bursts out into an exuberant expression of Greek references. It terminates eventually at 154 feet, providing the owner with a belvedere nearly a thousand feet above sea level.

The break between the plain shaft of the tower and the belvedere [48] is achieved through a deep Doric entablature with a boldly projecting cornice. The belvedere's three recessed windows add to the strong effect of *chiaroscuro*. Above the cornice surmounting the belvedere long panels of Greek key-fret decorate each face, and cubic blocks, ornamented with roundels, mark the corners. Decorative features of this sort are found in the work of Sir John Soane.

At this point the tower breaks from a square into a smaller, octagonal form, a shape reminiscent of the Tower of the Winds [49], illustrated in the first volume of *The Antiquities of Athens*.

48 The Lansdown Tower, belvedere

49 The Tower of the Winds, Athens

Such a reference would have certain relevance in this high, exposed and windy position. This upper, octagonal stage of the tower consists of two elements: a large stone base from which it rises, and, rising from it, a crowning lantern. The base is simply decorated with loopholes in the sides and urns upon the corners. The lantern, however, is far more interesting. It represents an octagonal version of the Choragic Monument of Lysicrates [50], a fanciful, circular building illustrated, again, in the first volume of *The Antiquities of Athens*.

The use of either of these Greek buildings as sources for Greek Revival work was not new. Indeed, James Stuart himself had built versions of both at Shugborough in 1764 and 1770 respectively. More public and generally accessible was James Wyatt's Radcliffe Observatory at Oxford, completed in 1794 as a version of the Tower of the Winds. The circular form of the Choragic Monument of Lysicrates provided an ideal model for garden temples and

50 The Choragic Monument of Lysicrates, Athens (below left)

51 St Matthew, Brixton, London, bellcote
[48–51] The belvedere at H E Goodridge's Lansdown Tower presents a fusion of the octagonal Tower of the Winds and the colonnaded Choragic Monument of Lysicrates, both illustrated in the first volume of James Stuart and Nicholas Revett's *Antiquities of Athens*. Such a combination had been tried but three times before, and then only in London churches, of which one was C F Porden's St Matthew, Brixton, of 1822–24.

funerary monuments up and down the country; as a bellcote it appeared at St John's Chapel in Chichester, built in 1812–13 to the designs of James Elmes, whose son Harvey Lonsdale Elmes was to be an assistant in Goodridge's Bath office between 1834 and 1837. What could be an early interpretation of the Choragic Monument can be found in Bath – the watchman's hut erected in 1793 at Norfolk Crescent [16].

It was the combination of the Tower of the Winds and the Choragic Monument of Lysicrates demonstrated by Goodridge at Lansdown Tower which was new and thoroughly up to date. Only three earlier examples are known and all are in London: W and H W Inwood's St Pancras New Church (1819–22), C F Porden's St Matthew's, Brixton (1822–24) [51] and F Bedford's St Luke, West Norwood (1823–25). A connection runs through all these architects: Porden supervised the building of St Pancras New Church for the Inwoods and served his articles with his uncle William Porden, through whom he might well have met Bedford, six years his elder and probably also a student of William Porden, of whose will he was later an executor. Goodridge seems to have had no connection with this circle and his interpretation of these Greek forms was the first example of their combined use both in a secular situation and outside London.

How Goodridge alighted upon this combination of precedents is difficult to say. He might well have been familiar with the new churches of London. But it is the fusion of the apparently Greek forms with the more weighty Tuscan villa architecture which is intriguing. It is known that Goodridge visited Italy in 1829: maybe he had been there before, perhaps as an extension of his visit to France of c1818. Some of his Italianate work on Bathwick Hill pre-dates 1829 and the Italian influence is also strong here at Lansdown. Had John Ruskin, in later years, seen the tower, he surely would have admired it as an illuminating expression of 'The Lamp of Power', for it rises quite sheer and unencumbered from the lower building. In this it is very much the Italian *campanile* and is at once reminiscent of the great tower at the Palazzo Scaligeri at Verona. Here a tall square tower is capped with an octagonal lantern and the break between the two stages is achieved through the use of a deep cornice, much as Goodridge did at Lansdown. Such a strong north Italian connection would not have been inappropriate at Lansdown where at the rear of the building, behind the tower, Beckford had Goodridge build him a small, apsidal oratory to St Anthony of Padua.

Whatever its provenance, Goodridge's Lansdown Tower remains a milestone in the development of Neo-Classicism in Britain. It is a unique combination of variant themes – Greek and Italian, the broken Picturesque and the powerful Sublime. It fuses geometry with nature and Classicism with Romanticism. It was never done again.

The clean, archaeological precedent of *The Antiquities of Athens*, once tried at Lansdown, proved a useful source for Goodridge's other work in Bath. Following on from the Lansdown Tower, his next major commission was for the building of the new bridge, now called Cleveland Bridge, which linked the developing Darlington Estatess south of the avon with the london road.

As early as 1810 James Goodridge, in his capacity as agent to the Darlington Estate, had been involved in negotiations for a bridge, designed by John Pinch, to be built over the Avon at Walcot. But negotiations had fallen through and nothing much more had happened until 1822 when Pinch, now in partnership with his son, also John Pinch, produced four new designs. Two were strongly rusticated, Classical affairs, not unlike the 1810 design, and were estimated at some £9,500 to £12,100. But more interesting, in this context, were the two cheaper designs which were for cast iron bridges and were to cost about £8,500 and £6,600. The first was to be a single cast iron span, the other a double span. Again, they were not built; nor were the alternative designs provided by two London engineers then at the top of their profession – John Rennie, who built Waterloo Bridge, London (1811–17) and Thomas Telford who built the Menai Straits Suspension Bridge (1819–26).

When the bridge was completed in 1827, to the designs of H E Goodridge, it was not dissimilar to the Pinch partnership's single span, cast iron design of five years earlier. Now this raises an interesting question. The elder Pinch's work in wrought iron at Norfolk Crescent and New Sydney Place has already been mentioned: he also used wrought iron balconies on all his terraces, and later the younger Pinch was to use cast iron balusters in the stairs of the Reference Library on Queen Square. Meanwhile Goodridge's wrought iron balconies at Woodland Place [52], being drawn without doubt from L N Cottingham's *Ornamental Metalworkers Director* (1823) [53], and his others at nos. 6 and 9 Cleveland Place West [54, 55], did not necessarily follow Pinch's but expressed the same lightness of touch. His heavier, cast iron work, as in Cleveland Bridge [56] and the stair balusters in his own

52 6 Woodland Place, balcony railings

53 Wrought-iron designs

house, Fiesole [57] on Bathwick Hill, actually employed floral medallions very similar to the younger Pinch's in the Reference Library stairs. It is clear that Goodridge had developed a fondness for ironwork – his further use of it in the porticoed entrance at no. 1 Lansdown Place West and in the railings around Beckford's tomb (which were later removed to the Lansdown Cemetery) are evidence of this. Did Goodridge develop this interest indepen-

54 6 Cleveland Place West, balcony railings

55 9 Cleveland Place West, balcony railings

dently or perhaps in collaboration with the Pinch partnership? Is it too much of a coincidence that both they and Goodridge produced designs for a cast iron bridge, the first just two years after Goodridge himself had set up in practice; that Goodridge's first large commission, the Argyle Chapel, bore a noticeable relationship to the elder Pinch's Sion Hill Place, then completing; and that Goodridge's father had worked with the same Pinch in the

56 Cleveland Bridge, balustrade

57 Fiesole, Bathwick Hill, stair baluster

[52–57] Cast and wrought-iron decoration, as illustrated in Lewis Nockalls Cottingham's *Ornamental Metalworkers Director* of 1823, lent themselves well to Greek Revival detailing and were extensively employed by H E Goodridge from this time onwards.

1810 attempt to get a bridge built? It would seem likely that after his apprenticeship with Lowder Goodridge worked, in one capacity or another, for Pinch, before Beckford picked him up.

There is none of the elder John Pinch in the stone toll-houses which flank the approaches to the Cleveland Bridge [58]. If anything there is Beckford's direction, so Greek are they – *tetrastyle* and Doric. For a source need Goodridge have looked any further than the first illustration of the first volume of *The Antiquities of Athens*? In adapting the design of this small Doric temple [59] he omits the triglyph, tenia and guttae from the frieze

58 Cleveland Bridge, toll-house

59 Doric portico, Athens

[58–59] H E Goodridge's toll-house for Cleveland Bridge of 1827 was derived from the first illustration in the first volume of James Stuart and Nicholas Revett's *Antiquities of Athens*.

60 The Bazaar, 9 Quiet Street   Probably built by H E Goodridge in 1824, the Bazaar draws upon both Greek and Roman sources, as interpreted variously by James Stuart and Nicholas Revett, and by Lord Burlington and also Robert Adam. The sculptural work, which includes the figures of Commerce and Genius on either side of the window, is by Lucius Gahagan.

and leaves the lower part of the columns unfluted. But otherwise it is all there, including the irregular spacing of the columns and the reinterpretation of the central acroterion, when seen in strict elevation, as a chimney.

Contemporary with these two designs, which leant so heavily upon *The Antiquities of Athens*, was the Auction Mart and Bazaar built in 1824 in Quiet Street. This work can only be attributed to Goodridge but the details, and their repetition at the Corridor, known to have been built by him in 1825, would make this likely.

The Bazaar, 9 Quiet Street [60], was unusual in that it was designed, with the flanking buildings, as commercial premises. The dominating central building is crowned by a broken and stepped parapet or blocking course which, being surmounted by a statue, is clearly borrowed from the Choragic Monument of Thrasyllus [61], shown in the second volume of *The Antiquities of Athens*. This monument on the steep side slopes of the Acropolis in Athens [62] is best viewed from close to and below, the only view of the Bazaar which the narrowness of Quiet Street affords.

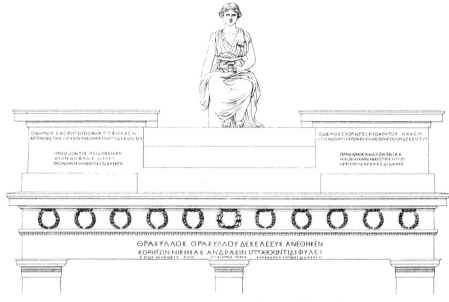

61 The Choragic Monument of Thrasyllus, Athens

62 The Choragic Monument of Thrasyllus, Athens

[61–62] The Bazaar's broken and stepped parapet or blocking course and its surmounting statue make a clear reference to the upper stage of the Choragic Monument of Thrasyllus, illustrated in James Stuart and Nicholas Revett's *Antiquities of Athens*.

Below the cornice, the great central window dominates the façade. Its form might be thought to be derived from Palladian or Venetian windows, but in these instances the central light is one with the round-headed opening above and the side lights remain as shorter, flanking openings. Yet here the architect carries the cornice and frieze right across the window, creating, in an abrupt manner, a divided arch with a three-light window below and a fanlight above.

The earliest English Palladian, Lord Burlington, had shown just such an arrangement in a sectional view taken through the Baths of Diocletian in Rome [63], which he illustrated in *Fabbriche Antiche Disegnate da Andrea Palladio* and published in 1730. He incorporated it the following year in his own design for the York Assembly Rooms [64], which was eventually illustrated in the fourth volume of *Vitruvius Britannicus* (1767). Yet there is a difference here in these thermae windows, in that the tripartite division is extended into the upper part of the opening. Although Issac Ware had picked this up and illustrated it in his *Complete Body of Architecture* (1756), no other architect seems to have used it to any degree until Robert Adam. Adam employed this window arrangement frequently – at the Adelphi [65] and Fitzroy Square [9] in London, and in the shop fronts on Pulteney Bridge [66] in Bath, where the semicircular upper part of the opening remains undivided. In fact, this window became about the most commercial of all the Adam motifs. Thus its use at the Bazaar suggests a case of Adam survival – or possibly even *revival*. But it was not just the window, in this instance, which was reminiscent of Adam, but the whole context. Consider Adam's design for the Board Room for the Paymaster General and Commissioners of the Chelsea Hospital in Whitehall, London [67]. The design was published in 1775. The arrangement of the central bay of this building bears more than a passing resemblance to the Bazaar. Not only is the cornice which breaks the window continued across the façade, but the whole is surmounted by a dominant attic storey and sculptural group. If the Board Room was the Roman version, then the Bazaar was the Greek.

The decoration of the spandrels on either side of the arch, with medallions or roundels, was a Palladian feature much employed by Adam. Although not in evidence in the Whitehall building, this can be seen on the south side of Pulteney Bridge as well as in the Adelphi and in a number of his published works. So it is not surprising to find the spandrels of the Bazaar's great window thus

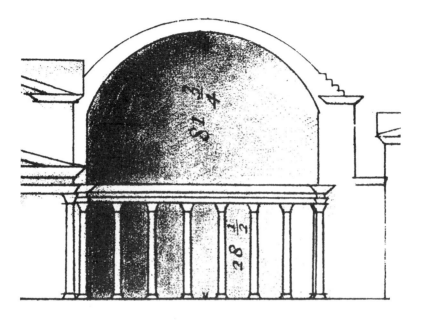

63 The Baths of Diocletian, Rome, cross-section

64 Assembly Rooms, York, elevation

65 The Adelphi, London
66 Pulteney Bridge

[63–66] The treatment of the great central window at the Bazaar is similar to that of the windows in Robert Adam's original design for Pulteney Bridge of 1769–74. Parallels can also be drawn to Adam's Adelphi, London, of 1768–72, where roundels highlight the spandrels of the arches as wreaths do at the Bazaar, and to his buildings on Fitzroy Square [9]. This method of subdividing round-headed openings with columns or pilasters and an entablature had been tried first by Lord Burlington at the York Assembly Rooms of 1731–32 and illustrated by him the previous year in his *Fabbriche Antiche Disegnate da Andrea Palladio*.

decorated. But again, the vocabulary is Greek and the decoration, appropriately derived from the Choragic Monument of Thrasyllus, is wreaths.

It is the wreaths which connect the Bazaar with the Corridor and other work known to be by Goodridge. Yet these and other features were popular in domestic and street architecture at the time and it would be wrong to think of Goodridge as the only

67 Board Room for the Paymaster General and the Commissioners of the Chelsea Hospital, London   If the Bazaar was based on any one building, it was probably this design published in *The Works in Architecture of Robert and James Adam*, but now heavily overworked with Greek imagery.

exponent of this style working in Bath. The great influence on the young men of the day was the eccentric old Professor of Architecture at the Royal Academy, Sir John Soane.

Soane had learnt much of his restrained, almost abstract Classicism under his master George Dance, some of which can be detected in Dance's Beauford Square façade of the Theatre Royal in Bath [23]. Soane's *tour de force* was his own London house at 13 Lincoln's Inn Fields (1812), and it was here that he had his office where, during his long career, he employed no less than twenty-nine pupils. J M Gandy was his principal assistant, but another, G A Underwood, already mentioned for rebuilding the Lower Assembly Rooms after the fire of 1820, was resident in Bath throughout the 1820s. Among Soane's pupils was Edward Davis, described by the master as 'a modest, unassuming young man', who came to live in Bath in about 1827 following his articles. And at about this time Soane, accompanied by his secretary George Wightwick, visited Beckford in Bath.

Soane's street architecture was idiosyncratic: it consisted largely of abstract, geometrical decoration, laced with Classical and often funerary references and articulated in the most subtle way. It was a style he established early in his life and which changed little over the years. Thus there were many sources for the young Bath architects to turn to, but here one must suffice: the shops and houses at 156–172 Regent Street, London [68], built in 1820 and published in Thomas Shepherd's *Metropolitan Improvements* of 1829. This building achieved some notoriety, for Soane, taking offence at the critic who accused him of the crime of trying to invent a new Order of architecture, brought an action for libel.

The most noticeable feature of the elevation is the manner in which columns and even pilasters have been replaced by vertical strips decorated with incised mouldings. The same method of decoration is picked up in the Greek key pattern of the frieze and the stylised volutes of the porch capitals. Such incised decoration had already been noticed in the upper stages of the Lansdown Tower. Goodridge was to use it again in c1829 at no. 9 Cleveland Place West [69], in what would have been the central house on the west side of his grand approach to Cleveland Bridge. Here is a familiar theme which is not apparent in Soane's Regent Street building – the wreath. A wreath decorates this central façade, and appears again surrounding small bull's eye windows in the attic storey of no. 2 Cleveland Place East opposite. Wreaths also play an important decorative role in the treatment of the Corridor running between Union Street and High Street [70]. This was built as a speculation by Goodridge in 1825. The High Street facade, opposite the Guildhall, is decorated by a large wreath set above the attic storey and here there is the second major reference to Soane's Regent Street building.

Set into the attic storey of the Corridor, and resting upon the cornice, are three semi-circular windows. The Regent Street building has similar, if rather more grand windows in the same location. With the exception of the wreath the skyline of the Corridor remains undecorated; Soane's skyline is decorated with a pierced balustrade, great, anthemia-like half shells set between volutes, and his favourite sarcophogal forms, cubes with rounded tops.

Such sarcophogal forms are used by Goodridge as capitals to the gate posts at Woodland Place on Bathwick Hill (c1834) [71], a scheme in which Harvey Lonsdale Elmes, Goodridge's assistant and later architect of St George's Hall, Liverpool, was almost certainly involved. Here too, on the corners of the terrace, are anthemia such as can be seen in the end porches at Regent Street. They appear again in two other buildings that could well be by Goodridge – the (Berni) Royal and Argyll Hotels opposite Bath Spa Station.

Goodridge was employed as surveyor to the Great Western Railway and it would seem likely that he built one if not both of these hotels in the early 1840s, soon after the railway came to Bath. In fact Manvers Street was laid out in accordance with precise instructions contained in the 1835 Great Western Railway Act. It is the Argyll Hotel [72] which displays the familiar vocabulary – the anthemia, the wreaths along the ground floor frieze and, on the Manvers Street and Railway Place façades, windows such as at the Bazaar, but now with the fanlight blind, as at Cleveland Place East – and perhaps the (Berni) Royal Hotel is a copy. The striking feature which both these hotels share is the way in which they move around the corner. This is done simply and effectively by placing, at first and second floor level, Giant Order Ionic columns, *distyle-in-antis*. With this simple device, held between a solid podium and a heavy attic, the building addresses and controls the corner, giving equal importance to each adjacent façade. It had been done before, although in a Corinthian Order, at the Bank of England. The architect there was Sir John Soane.

The extent of Soane's relationship to the architecture of Bath is intriguing. Many references to his work are apparent. Perhaps the

68 156–172 Regent Street, London

69 9 Cleveland Place West

70 The Corridor, High Street

71 Woodland Place
[68–71] The stripped and abstracted Classicism of Sir John Soane's architecture, such as his 1820 terrace in Regent Street, London, provided a model for later building in Bath, including H E Goodridge's Cleveland Place West of c1829, the corridor of 1825 and Woodland Place of c1834.

72 The Argyll Hotel and the (Berni) Royal Hotel, Manvers Street   Built in the early 1840s, the Argyll and (Berni) Royal Hotels, which were probably by H E Goodridge, recall the London architecture of Sir John Soane as well as the Bazaar and other Bath buildings by Goodridge.

most unexpected can be seen at Smallcombe Grove, now Oakwood, built on Bathwick Hill in c1830. Considering both its Italianate appearance and its location, adjacent to Woodland Place, one would suspect the earlier part of the building to be by Goodridge. The later, yet rather more Soanesque part [73], was added in c1850 by William Bruce Gingell, a Bath-trained Bristol architect. So was it Gingell or Goodridge who designed the dining room ceiling in the older part of the house? For it is a thin, quasi-Gothic starfish ceiling, just as Soane had created for himself in his breakfast room at Lincoln's Inn Fields [74] in 1792–4 and also at his country house, Pitzhanger Manor at Ealing. Nearer to Bath, another such ceiling was built above the grand staircase at Longleat House by Sir Jeffrey Wyatville in 1806–13.

73 Smallcombe Lodge, Bathwick Hill
74 12 Lincoln's Inn Fields, London, the breakfast room

[73–74] The influence of Sir John Soane is apparent in William Bruce Gingell's extension of c1850 to Smallcombe Lodge (now Oakwood) and also in the dining room located in the older part of the house beyond. This room, with its starfish ceiling, is very similar to the breakfast room Soane built for himself at 12 Lincoln's Inn Fields, London, in 1792–94. Since the older part of Smallcombe Lodge is most likely by H E Goodridge, could he have designed the dining room?

THE IMPERIAL ROMAN REVIVAL

In the enthusiasm for Neo-Classicism which swept European architecture during the early years of the nineteenth century the British sought their sources in ancient Greece, while the French sought theirs in Rome. Imperial Rome, an expression of power, was probably closer to Napoleon's way of thinking than stoic Greece, where the perfection of art lay in simplicity. There are really two reasons for this polarisation: the first is one of nationalism – the British could not be seen to be following the lead given by the French, and thus turned to the Levant. The second, and architecturally the more relevant reason, was that in the move away from Palladianism Roman architecture was, by association, also rejected.

It is therefore surprising to find two noticeably Roman designs built in Bath during the first half of the nineteenth century – remember that the Roman Baths, in their extensiveness, had still to be discovered. And it would follow, as might be expected, that the immediate source for one of these had been built in eighteenth-century Paris.

The first of these two buildings to be finished was the Moravian Chapel [75], more recently the Christian Science Church, in Charlotte Street. It was designed in 1845 by a young Bath architect, James Wilson, whose prominently placed church of St Stephen on Lansdown was then just completing. The site he was given in Charlotte Street provided just one frontage and was hemmed in by houses to the west and the new Bath Savings Bank (now the Registry Office) to the east. Nevertheless, Wilson's façade is hardly timid.

The dominant feature of the building is the portico, a great triangular pediment above a deep frieze, supported on paired Corinthian columns. The whole composition owes much to the work of Sir John Vanbrugh and Nicholas Hawksmoor. The use of paired columns on either side of a portico is a hallmark of Vanbrugh and was much used by Hawksmoor. It can be seen in their collaborative work at Blenheim Palace, Oxfordshire (1705–

25): square and round columns in Hawksmoor's colonnade to the kitchen court [76] and double square columns in Vanbrugh's north portico, where the columns support a great pediment on a modillioned cornice and deep frieze, such as Wilson was to do at Charlotte Street. An illustration in the second volume of *Vitruvius Britannicus* [77], takes the relationship further. Vanbrugh's new design for Eastbury shows, as well as paired columns on either side of the portico, round and flat-arched flanking windows which could have provided a basis for Wilson's design.

But this is all English Baroque, architecturally a generation or two removed from Imperial Rome, where the paired columns and the powerful composition had their origin. Much more Neo-Classical and, indeed, nearer home, was the portico which James Wyatt had added onto the garden façade of Doddington House in Gloucestershire between 1798 and 1813. Here, once again, square and round columns flank the entrance.

The exact reproduction of Roman detail at the Moravian Chapel is found, however, in the capitals. They are of a distinctive, Corinthian Order and come, with little doubt, from the Temple of Vesta at Tivoli [78]. The six-petal flower set between volutes cannot be mistaken, although the original has been interpreted variously. It is likely that Wilson's source was George Ledwell Taylor and Edward Cresy's *The Architectural Antiquities of Rome*, published in 1821, which contained detailed drawings of the Temple. Yet the capital was as far as Wilson chose to go in his borrowings, for at Tivoli the columns are fluted and the frieze heavily decorated. Wilson kept his elevation bold and plain while, incidentally, stealing a little from the neighbouring Savings Bank in his treatment of the quoins.

The second expedition into Roman architecture in Bath is, by comparison, far less well known. Yet it is described by Pevsner as 'the most impressive church interior of its date in the country'. It is the Roman Catholic church of St Paul at Prior Park. Although designed in 1844 – the original interior drawing by the architect Joseph John Scoles hangs in the church [79] – the building was not consecrated until 1882. As a design it was, in 1844, remarkable, but by the time of its completion, nearly forty years later, it had been eclipsed.

Bishop Peter Augustine Baines had bought Prior Park, Ralph Allen's old house (after William Beckford had considered it too expensive) in the year of Roman Catholic emancipation, 1829. It was his intention to use the building as a seminary for the Western

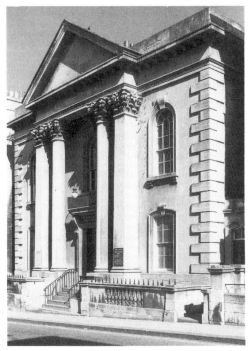

75 The Moravian Church, Charlotte Street

76 Blenheim Palace, Oxfordshire

77 'House in Dorset', later Eastbury Park

Vicarate, and in 1830 Baines installed himself there with four monks and twenty one students. It was his wish to build a great church which, as the centre of the college, would dominate the main house. Even though Goodridge prepared designs for a domed building this was not to be, for Baines died suddenly in the summer of 1843.

Almost immediately Scoles, himself a Roman Catholic, was commissioned to provide designs for a church to act, presumably, both as a memorial to Baines and to service the seminary. But the Vicarate was the poorest in England and the college was in a penurious state. All the same, the great west wing was soon demolished and work started on the foundation. There was an ·elderly Roman Catholic woman, a Miss Bettington, who insisted that the church be built, and before she died, so that she might be buried in a vault beneath it. She provided £2,000 and a further

78 The Temple of Vesta, Tivoli, capital

[75–78] James Wilson's Moravian Church of 1845 draws, in its heavy portico, upon Sir John Vanbrugh's work at Blenheim Palace of 1722–25 and Eastbury Park of 1718, the latter published in Colen Campbell's *Vitruvius Britannicus*. Its petalled capitals come from the Temple of Vesta at Tivoli, which had been illustrated, twenty-two years earlier, in George Ledwell Taylor and Edward Cresy's *The Architectural Antiquities of Rome*.

79 St Paul, Prior Park, interior

£1,000 came from a priest in Birmingham. But then, when the walls and columns were raised to the height of the cornice, the funds ran out. By 1847, the College had debts of £60,000 and assets of only £40,000. The end came in 1856, when the College and its effects were sold by auction for £6,832.

Eleven years later it was repurchased by William Clifford, the new Bishop of Clifton, to provide new premises for the Clifton Catholic Grammar School. Clifford, the younger brother of Baron Clifford of Chudleigh, was well connected and had the great ability of attracting generous benefactors and, once the school was established, set to work on completing the church which was now overgrown and apparently ruinous. It was on the day of Clifford's silver jubilee as Bishop, 6 July 1882, that St Paul's Church was opened and high mass said for the first time. But Scoles had been dead nearly twenty years and his church was far surpassed in magnificence by Herbert Gribble's new Brompton Oratory in London (1880). St Paul's has never been finished, and now it is unlikely to be. High up on the walls blocks of stone still wait to be carved into Corinthian capitals [80] and the panels around the apse remain naked of the paintings Scoles envisaged. Yet what is there is, for a design of 1844, extraordinary. It is not only stylistically innovative but dominates, in scale, the Palladian of the main house and the Greek Doric of the nearby Ball Court, built in 1841 by Goodridge. Now this building, with its eighty foot colonnade of twelve Doric columns *in antis* is heavily scaled and open to the sky. Yet Scoles' St Paul's, so long open to the sky [81] in its unfinished state, outscaled even the Greek Doric of that other rather enigmatic structure.

There was no connection between J J Scoles and the West Country – nor, indeed, should there be – but, as the leading Roman Catholic church architect of the time, with perhaps the exception of Pugin, to whom the Palladian Prior Park would have been anathema in any case, Scoles was the natural choice of architect. As a young man, in the early 1820s, he had travelled extensively both

80 St Paul, Prior Park

81 St Paul, Prior Park, incomplete interior

82 St Paul, Prior Park, interior

83 St Philippe du Roule, Paris, interior

[79–83] Started in 1844, John Joseph Scoles' Napoleonically-scaled church of St Paul has never been completed, but its intention, as indicated in Scoles' perspective, has been achieved. The building stood as a shell for over thirty years before it was consecrated in 1882. Even though unfinished – note the exterior capitals – it is, as Pevsner remarks, 'the most impressive church interior of its date in the country' and, as such, is clearly derived from Jean-François-Therese Chalgrin's St Philippe du Roule, built in Paris in 1768–84.

on the Continent and in the Levant, and it is in Paris that the most immediate inspiration for his design can be seen.

The interior of St Paul's [82] is derived unequivocally from the church of St Philippe du Roule in Paris [83], built by Jean-François-Therese Chalgrin, better known for his Arc de Triomphe. Chalgrin had designed St Philippe du Roule in 1768, yet it was not completed until 1784. Meanwhile, work was proceeding on the second building which was to have a bearing on Scoles' design, Jacques-Ange Gabriel's chapel at the Ecole Militaire at Paris. St Paul's is a combination of these two buildings. From St Philippe du Roule, Scoles took the overall arrangement; the basilica with side aisles, the rounded apse and the coffered barrel vault. From the Ecole Militaire came the Giant Order, fluted, Corinthian columns and the huge entablature. St Philippe du Roule, by comparison, was Ionic.

The basilica is a Roman form and its use in combination with

Giant Order, probably Corinthian columns, separating the aisles, comes straight from the fifth book of Vitruvius' *Treatise on Architecture*. In this book he describes his own design for a basilica at Fano in north Italy but, since no trace of that building has remained, details of the design have been difficult to confirm. It is likely, however, that the French architects turned to a source nearer home for their own precedents. The Temple of Diana at Nimes in the south of France (second century AD) is a basilica-like space with a ribbed, barrel vaulted ceiling rising from a bold entablature, supported on engaged Corinthian or Composite columns, which encircled the space. Although partly ruinous, much of the original form of this building remains. For his smoothly coffered ceiling Chalgrin could have used any number of sources from Piranesi to the Pantheon at Rome. Scoles, however, might well have seen the remains of the Temple of Jupiter at Baalbek in the Lebanon (first century AD) where the ribbed and coffered ceiling is very close to what he did at St Paul's. And this really begs the question: could Scoles actually have by-passed the more obvious sources of Chalgrin and Gabriel and gone straight to what they, perhaps unknowingly, were emulating?

It is perhaps worth noting here, even parenthetically, that Decimus Burton's designs for the Tepid Bath in Stall Street also employed a basilica plan. In the context of Roman baths, this would seem to be appropriate. Burton, whose Athenaeum in London's Pall Mall was then under construction, was called in by the city in 1829 to advise on improving the baths. Yet, in the end, what Ison describes as Burton's 'impeccably Classical design' was actually built by the city architect in 1830, only to be demolished barely a hundred years later in 1923. Thankfully, Burton's architecture elsewhere has fared rather better.

It is perhaps worth noting here, even parenthetically, that Decimus Burton's designs for the Tepid Bath in Stall Street also employed a basilica plan. In the context of Roman baths, this would seem to be appropriate. Burton, whose Athenaeum in London's Pall Mall was then under construction, was called in by the city in 1829 to advise on improving the baths. Yet, in the end, what Ison describes as Burton's 'impeccably Classical design' was actually built by the city architect in 1830, only to be demolished barely a hundred years later in 1923. Thankfully, Burton's architecture elsewhere has fared rather better.

CHAPTER 4

Picturesque Architecture and the Landscape

THE CULT OF THE PICTURESQUE

In the picture of *Cephalus and Procris* [84], painted by Claude Lorraine in 1645 and now held at the National Gallery in London, the two lovers, shown in the Roman *campagna*, are being reunited by the goddess Diana. This classical trio serves as a reminder, much as the ruined buildings do, of the continuing presence of antiquity in the landscape. The effect of the scene was emotional and, being worked through the medium of a picture, became referred to as Picturesque. What the word now conjures up is a certain informal relationship between man and his landscape, and these ideas developed as an attitude in England towards the end of the eighteenth century. Thus the relationship of buildings to the landscape and the cult of the Picturesque were by no means new when William Beckford built his tower up on Lansdown.

At the beginning of the eighteenth century Sir John Vanbrugh had shown, when he created Blenheim Palace, how great architecture could work at one with the landscape. Here the broken Baroque skyline of the Palace merged well with the surrounding parkland, later landscaped by Capability Brown. With the building of Richard Payne Knight's Downton Castle in Herefordshire in 1772 the Picturesque in architecture took on a new interpretation. Downton Castle was a thoroughly irregular, castellated pile and suggested the relationship between Romanticism and the Picturesque. This was immediately developed by Robert Adam at Culzean Castle, Ayrshire (1777–92) and then by other architects working noticeably in Scotland – for example, the London architect Robert Lugar, who built Tullichewan Castle in

84 Claude Lorraine, *Cephalus and Procris*   Claude's painting of 1645, now in the National Gallery, London, provides the perfect expression of the Italian *campagna*.

Dumbartonshire (1808). Even the Woods dabbled in this castle style, as drawings held at the Bath Reference Library indicate, but with the exception of the rather unconvincing castle at Tregenna near St Ives in Cornwall, built by the younger Wood in 1773–74, their ideas remained on paper.

Thus, in the early years of the nineteenth century there was a tendency to interpret the Picturesque as Romanticism: the vastly popular Waverley Novels of Sir Walter Scott only encouraged this. The interpretation of the Picturesque as antique, as opposed to Romantic, had been demonstrated often in painting, but not really in architecture. The early Greek Revival, as has been intimated, initially did nothing more than provide gazebos and gewgaws for the English country parks. The breakthrough which allowed monumental Classical architecture to work at one with the landscape came with William Wilkins' great house in Hampshire, The Grange (1809). When Charles Robert Cockerell first visited Grange Park in 1823 he was enraptured. 'Nothing' he said, 'can be finer, more classical or like the finest Poussino, it realises the most fanciful representations of the painters pencil or the poet's description.' This was the real value of The Grange.

Bath is fortunate in possessing, on the very edge of the city, a perfect example of the eighteenth-century English landscaped park – Prior Park. Designed by the elder Wood for Ralph Allen and built by Wood and Richard Jones, Allen's clerk of works, between 1735 and c1750, the house was probably the most ambitious recreation of a Palladian house in England. The park it addresses was laid out purely for scenic effect: the valley is too steep for cultivation and the flat bottom is filled with a lake. The city which can now be seen rising up across the valley, on the far northern hills, is of our century: originally green hills would have formed a backdrop to the landscape, perhaps with glimpses of the smart metropolitan improvements to the old medieval city beyond. Three themes in landscape gardening had been prevalent in the eighteenth century: the traditional but soon outdated axial layout; the more ornamental Chinese garden proposed rather facetiously by Sir William Chambers; and the irregular but carefully controlled landscape of Lancelot 'Capability' Brown. Although there is no evidence to suggest it is by Brown himself, Prior Park is an example of the last of these.

Prior Park has all the elements of a Capability Brown landscape. The trees were arranged in belts and clumps controlling the views which, at the bottom of the valley, alighted upon the lake, developed out of some old monastic fishponds. The steep sides of the valley were grassed and kept in trim by the occasional sheep. Set romantically beside the lake was the Palladian Bridge, which was modelled on one built at Wilton in 1736. But the aesthete of the late eighteenth century would have viewed such a landscape as this with contempt. It was to his mind as artificial as the axial forms which had preceded it. Capability Brown's landscapes, for all their apparent irregularity, were controlled and nature was harnessed.

The cult of the Picturesque was born in 1794–5. Its thesis was argued out in three books, Richard Payne Knight's *The Landscape, a Didactic Poem* (1794), Uvedale Price's *Essay on the Picturesque* (1794) and Humphrey Repton's *Sketches and Hints on Landscape Gardening* (1794). Their contention was that raw nature should be respected far more than it ever was in Capability Brown's work. In this at least they all agreed, and this standard proved to be the basis of the Picturesque.

The new, metropolitan city of Bath allowed raw nature no scope and in his *Essay on the Picturesque* Price recorded his impression on first seeing the city:

> I remember my disappointment the first time I approached Bath, notwithstanding the beauty of the stone with which it is built, and of many of the parts on a nearer view. Whoever considers what are the forms of the summits, how little the buildings are made to yield to the ground, and how few trees are mixed with them, will account for my disappointment, and probably lament the cause of it.

This change of attitude was soon addressed, and thus popularised, in a now well-known piece in Jane Austen's *Northanger Abbey*. Although published posthumously in 1818, this passage was probably written prior to 1803, thus making it absolutely contemporary with the development of the cult of the Picturesque. The scene is set at Beechen Cliff, 'that noble hill, whose beautiful verdure and hanging coppice render it so striking an object from almost every opening in Bath'. The young Catherine Moreland is considering the outlook in the erudite company of Eleanor and Henry Tilney:

> The Tilneys . . . were viewing the country with the eyes of persons accustomed to drawing, and decided on its

capability of being formed into pictures, with all the eagerness of real taste. Here Catherine was quite lost. She knew nothing of drawing – nothing of taste: - and she listened to them with an attention which brought her little profit, for they talked in phrases which conveyed scarcely any idea to her. The little which she could understand however appeared to contradict the very notions she had entertained on the matter before. It seemed as if a good view were no longer to be taken from the top of a high hill, and that a clear blue sky was no longer proof of a fine day. . . He talked of fore-grounds, distances, and second distances – side-screens and perspectives – lights and shades; - and Catherine was so hopeful a scholar, that when they gained the top of Beechen Cliff, she voluntarily rejected the whole city of Bath, as unworthy to make part of a landscape.

BECKFORD'S WALK

It was nature, raw and unbridled, which provided the backbone of William Beckford's walk along the upper length of Lansdown [85]. In 1822 Lansdown Crescent lay on the northern extremity of the city and behind it stretched a hillside of arable land, rough pastures and disused quarries. There was but one farm, Moger's, and a number of farm buildings. The situation offered Beckford the opportunity to try every landscape trick in the book. The result was a dramatic progression from the enclosed and formal to the open and wild. Where trees were lacking he brought them in, but there is none of the contrived control of the Capability Brown landscape.

It can be assumed without doubt that it was H E Goodridge who planned the architectural features along the walk, although doubtless he was assisted horticulturally by Vincent, Beckford's head gardener from Fonthill. Since Goodridge's work can be seen at the start and termination of the walk, his involvement with its layout would have seemed likely; the similarity between the embattled gateway and the 'Saxon' design for the tower, and Edward English's illustration of the gateway together with his acknowledgement of Goodridge in his 1844 folio volume of *Views of Lansdown Tower*, would seem to confirm it.

Beckford's landscape ran from the Romantic to the Sublime, from the formal to the wild. The walk started from the garden at the

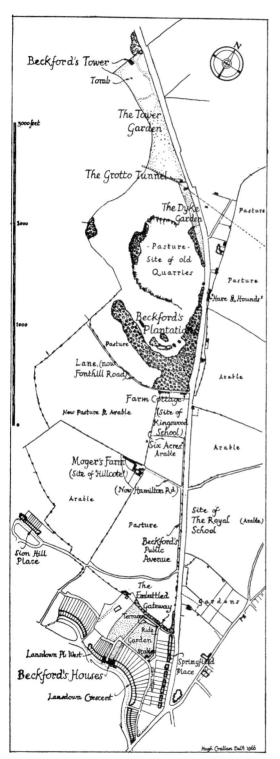

Beckford's Tower

Tomb

The Tower Garden

The Grotto Tunnel

The Dyke Garden

Pasture

-Pasture-
Site of old Quarries

Pasture

"Hare & Hounds"

Beckford's Plantation

Pasture

Arable

Lane, (now Fonthill Road)

Farm Cottage

New Pasture & Arable

(Site of Kingswood School)

"Six Acres" Arable

Arable

Moger's Farm (Site of 'Hillcote')

(Now Hamilton Rd)

Arable

Site of The Royal School   (Arable)

Pasture

Beckford's Public Avenue

Sion Hill Place

The Embattled Gateway

Gardens

Terrace

Ride Garden Stables

Lansdown Pl West

Beckford's Houses

Springfield Place

Lansdown Crescent

3000 feet

2000

1000

Hugh Crallan Delt 1966

85 Beckford's Walk, Lansdown, plan
Beckford's Walk, laid out between 1825
and 1838, was punctuated with
architectural features designed
by H E Goodridge, and ran from
20 Lansdown Crescent to the
Lansdown Tower

rear of no. 20 Lansdown Crescent, at the far end of which, by the gate to the mews, Beckford had a small, mosque-like Islamic pavilion built [86]: perhaps a last backward glance to his novel from Fonthill, *Vathek*, or just a demonstration of the Romantic. Across the mews, behind the Crescent, in an area of about four acres, he planted his kitchen garden. Here, on the east side, beneath a massive rampart, were the stables. These ramparts and the terraces which formed the other side of the garden remain today, but the space between has recently produced a harvest of houses. High above the garden, at the top of the rampart, was the embattled gateway [87] which marked the start of the pathway across open country.

The path ran through fields, now built over, past Moger's farm and the 'six acres arable' which later bore Kingswood School, and into the plantation above Fonthill Road. It was from here that the view was the most breathtaking. In an attempt to maintain his privacy Beckford managed to obtain permission to close off a number of public footpaths in this part of the walk: but he was required to provide an alternative public route. This remains today, the 12 foot wide grassed avenue, formerly gravel, which runs along the side of Lansdown Road from Sion Road to beyond Hamilton Road. Twenty one of the original lime trees survive.

Beyond the plantations the walk opened out onto a craggy plateau where there were the quarries which had provided stone for the city below. 'The remains of these quarries,' wrote the landscape painter Henry Venn Lansdown in 1838, 'are most picturesque. At a little distance they seem to present the wrecks of stately buildings, the rows of broken arches, and vividly recall the idea of Roman ruins. I afterwards mentioned my impressions on seeing them to Mr Beckford who replied, "They do indeed put one in mind of the Campagna of Rome, and are vastly like the ruins of the Baths of Caracalla" '. Such a landscape is worthy of Claude or Poussin.

After the openness of the plateau, the intensity of the second, smaller plantation was severe. Lansdown continued his description: 'We quitted the open Down, and passing under a low doorway entered a lovely shrubbery. The walk (composed of small fossils) winds between graceful trees, and is skirted by odoriferous flowers, which we are astonished to find growing in such luxuriance at an elevation of nearly a thousand feet above the vale below. In many places the trees meet, and form a green arcade over your head, whilst patches of mignonette, giant plants of

86 Islamic Pavilion, 20 Lansdown Crescent

heliotrope, and clusters of geranium perfume the air.' Thus the contrast could hardly have been more acute and the use of a low doorway particularly effective.

At the far end, through another doorway, was the Dyke Garden. It was a kitchen garden, long and narrow, with a broad, grassed path down its centre and, being formed in an old quarry, was well

87 Embattled Gateway, Lansdown [86–87] H E Goodridge's Islamic Pavilion marked the start of Beckford's Walk and the Embattled Gateway, decorated with Beckford's arms, was located where the Walk emerged into open country.

sheltered. Once again the contrast of spaces was acute. This Lansdown recalled, 'One cannot describe one's sensations of comfort at finding so delicious a spot in so unexpected a place. I said to the gardener, "I understand Mr Beckford had planted everything on the Down, but you surely found these apple trees here. They are fifty years old." "We found nothing here but an old quarry and a few nettles. Those apple trees were great trees when we moved them, and moving them stopped their bearing. They blossom in the spring and look pretty, and that is all Master cares about." ' The far end of the garden was masked with an Italianate building, through the centre of which passed an archway, recalling the allusion to the *campagna*.

The walk now passed under the lane that led to Chelscombe Farm, opposite to where Granville Road now joins Lansdown Road at Endsleigh. Here beside 'a pond of gold and silver fish' Beckford built a grotto, reminiscent of that at Stourhead (1748 and 1776), a tunnel which ran for some seventy feet to rustic steps which led out again onto the Down. This end of the tunnel is all that remains, but the steps are now lost amid a tangle of brambles. 'Looking back,' Lansdown wrote, 'you cannot but admire the natural appearance of this work of art. . . There is nothing formed, nothing apparently artificial, and a young ash springs as if accidentally from between the stones.' This was unbridled nature of the true Picturesque.

The final stage of the walk, through the tower garden, wild and Picturesque to contrast with the Sublime mass of the tower, survived perhaps only until 1848 when the grounds became a cemetery. Evidence of the landscaping and planting, however, still remain. Although Picturesque features such as an archway and a ruin decorated the gardens it was the extraordinary variety of planting that amazed Lansdown. 'Shrubs and trees, whose natural climates are as opposite as the antipodes, here flourish in the most astonishing manner. We were shown a rose tree brought from Peking and a fir tree brought from the highest part of the Himalaya mountains . . . a tree that once vegetated in Larissa, in Greece, Italian pines, Siberian pines, Scotch firs, a lovely specimen of Irish yew, and other trees which it is impossible to describe. My astonishment was great at witnessing the size of the trees, and I could scarcely believe my ears when told that the whole of the wood had been raised on the bare down within the last thirteen years.'

Thus between 1825 and 1838 Beckford created a progression unique in landscape architecture. It was the evocation of many of the principles of Knight, Price and Repton, but it was also, in places, an expression of the more contemporary concept of the Gardenesque. This had been developed by J C Loudon who argued that, for a garden to be a work of art, it must be above nature: it should be so different from nature that it could not be mistaken for anything but a work of art. From Lansdown's description of the wide ranging collection of planting, we can see that the tower garden was just this. In such an enclosed space it could work, and most effectively. Beyond the garden, on the down, the greater landscape could not be so controlled and the acknowledged charm of the Repton School of the Picturesque was allowed to dominate. Thus the Gardenesque and the Picturesque were, ultimately, incompatible.

THE ROYAL VICTORIA PARK

While Beckford sought to maintain his privacy by closing off parts of Lansdown, a move was made by some leading citizens in 1829 to provide a public space of similar nature. The result was the Royal Victoria Park. The *Report On The Formation Of The Park*, published two years later, recalls the feeling: 'The spirit of the times demanded some additional attraction, particularly, that of Ornamental Plantations, Walks, and Rides being formed in our immediate Vicinity.' A rough plan therefore was drawn up in 1829 which formed the basis of the eventual design by the young Bath architect, Edward Davis. The chosen site was to the west of the Royal Crescent [88].

> To supply the deficiency complained of, the delightful meadows, called the Bath Commons, present a site at once possessing every advantage for such a purpose.

The Bath Commons were clearly very suitable. They were on a slight incline, faced south, and were within easy reach of the city centre. This more or less rectangular piece of land was to be dressed with a kidney shaped carriage-way leading from the one main entrance set just below Marlborough Buildings. This was to be laid out, appropriately enough, by the newly appointed surveyor of the Bath Turnpike Trust, William Macadam, the son of James Macadam. Further land on the slopes of Sion Hill to the north, just below Doric House, was to be connected by an extension of the carriage-way running underneath Julian Road which, at this point, assumed the status of a 'Proposed Viaduct'. To the east of Marlborough Lane, below the Royal Crescent, were the Crescent Fields owned by Lady Rivers. It was at her suggestion that a road, now Royal Avenue, was run along below the Royal Crescent from the north east end of Queen's Parade near Queen

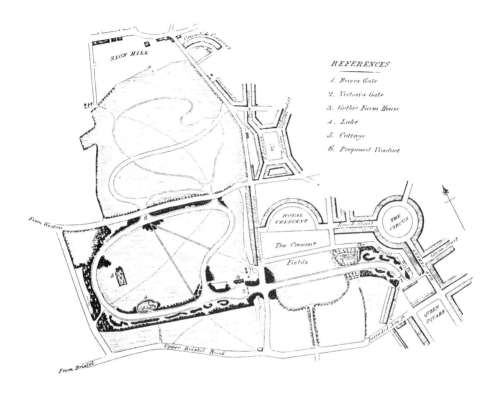

88 The Royal Victoria Park, plan

Square to a point on Marlborough Lane right across from the entrance to the park. Thus the gate by Queen's Parade is known as Rivers Gate, although it was erected some years later.

As well as a carriage-way, a lake and belt of trees, the park was to have a Gothic Farm House and a Cottage [89] which both served a very definite purpose in creating the required effect. Indeed, it was intended that the 'tasteful Gothic building . . . will present a most picturesque object in the general landscape'.

The placing of Gothic or other ornamental buildings in the landscape was, as has been indicated, a product of the English Picturesque movement. Often these were uninhabited – and uninhabitable, like Sham Castle on Claverton Down (1762) – but they were sometimes built for occupation by gardeners and other groundspeople, which is what Ralph Allen did for his Mr Dudsley at Prior Park in the early 1740s. It was John Nash who, at Blaise Hamlet at Henbury in Bristol, really changed this. Hitherto Nash, sometimes in association with Humphrey Repton, had built the occasional estate cottage, dairy, lodge and even villa, in the Picturesque Gothic style; but at Blaise Hamlet in 1810–11 Nash brought the themes together in a group of nine cottages in a field just below Blaise Castle. Even though these cottages were in the nature of an anthology, a number of the designs being reused from elsewhere, Nash demonstrated that the Gothic cottage could be more than just an ornamental extravagance, a mere dwelling for an agricultural labourer. It could be the basis of a residential community.

These *cottages ornées* as they are best referred to, prompted a whole series of publications in this vein. The first, John Buonarotti Papworth's *Rural Residences* (1818), was soon followed by Peter Frederick Robinson's *Rural Architecture, or a Series of Designs for*

89 The Royal Victoria Park, gateway and *cottage ornée*

[88–89] Edward Davis planned the Royal Victoria Park, on open land to the west of the Royal Crescent, in 1829. The gateway and *cottage ornée*, built by Davis in 1830, show the influence of his recent employer, Sir John Soane, and of the publications of John Buonarotti Papworth, and others, popular at that time.

Ornamental Cottages (1823) and *Designs for Ornamental Villas* (1825–27). The 1830s were dominated in this field by Charles Parker's long running monthly publication of Italianate designs, *Villa Rustica* (1832–41), and by the stream of works from J C Loudon. It was in the midst of this flurry of activity that Davis designed the buildings for the Royal Victoria Park.

Early prints of the Gothic Farm House in the park show a coy, thatched, diamond-lighted affair, lending itself wholeheartedly to the 'Shady Promenades and Agreeable Drives' that the city fathers were providing. Whether this was ever built or in later years was altered, is unclear. Nevertheless, the building that stands by the Victoria Gate is in the *ornée* tradition promulgated by Papworth and perpetuated by Loudon. It provides a strong contrast with the hard, geometrical forms of the gate itself.

Many examples of ornamental buildings and estate gateways survive from the work of Sir John Soane. When Davis joined Soane's office in Lincoln's Inn Fields the master was over seventy and his practice was contained almost exclusively within London. Yet Davis would have had the contents of that remarkable house from which to study and learn. While there, Soane was engaged on his last country house, Pellwall, near Market Drayton in Staffordshire (1822–28). Thus the severe and abstract forms of Davis' gateway [89], clearly derived from the classical triumphal arch, come as little surprise. A nice feature, now sadly rather mutilated, was the cast iron screen. The centre pier, all that remains, is cast with a vertical line of anthemia: as good an example of Greek Revival ironwork as that which can still be seen in the gates to Partis College.

Work on the park began in January 1830. The *Report* describing the work smacks rather of parochial self congratulation:

> A greater than usual number of labouring men were out of work ... it is satisfactory therefore to know, that the Improvements in the Bath Commons were the means of giving employment to nearly two hundred *inhabitants* during the winter months.

The alternative for these *inhabitants* might have been the parish charities. Within a year some '25,000 evergreens, forest trees, and shrubs' were well heeled in and 'the scattered streams of the field concentrated into a Pond, now form an ornamental Piece of Water of considerable extent and beauty.'

The 1831 *Report* on the formation of the Royal Victoria Park ends with a charming testimonial from the committee to their architect. It is worth quoting in full:

> The committee disclaim any participation in that just meed of praise so liberally bestowed – it belongs to Mr EDWARD DAVIS, and to him exclusively. He it is, who has in this instance, so happily blended the luxuriance of Nature, with the Classical proportions of Art, as to render the PARK at once an ornament to his native City, and a lasting memorial to his own fame.

The park was opened on 28 October 1830 by the Duchess of Kent and her daughter, Princess Victoria: thus it was known as the Royal Victoria Park.

The monument in honour of Victoria which was erected close to the gates in 1837 was not for the occasion of her succession but of her majority at the age of eighteen. The design, a triangular obelisk with three crouching lions and a balustrade surrounding, was by the long-serving city architect George Phillips Manners. An earlier published design, also by Manners, shows three spouting dolphins in place of the lions, the whole set amid a rocky pool enclosed by a low parapet wall.

Bath had something of a tradition of obelisks, the others being in the Orange Grove (1734) and in Queen Square (1738). Although no obelisk had been erected for a century, it is possible that the impetus for this new one at Bath was provided by the national competition for the Nelson Column in Trafalgar Square, London (erected 1839–42): James Wilson, for one, had entered.

One later development in the park is worth chronicling, although it hardly relates to the Picturesque. The Crystal Palace, built in London's Hyde Park in 1851, had demonstrated a new use for the cast-iron and glass architecture of the hot-house. With the removal of the Crystal Palace from Hyde Park to Sydenham in 1852, the true value· of the temporary nature of this type of construction was realised. In 1857, the year in which the South Kensington Museum – another glass and cast iron structure known derogatively as the Brompton Boilers – was opened, a prospectus was issued for a Music Hall and Winter Garden to be built in the Royal Victoria Park [90]. The building was of glass and cast iron, and the design probably by James Wilson. The previous year Wilson had drawn up a large perspective design for a Winter

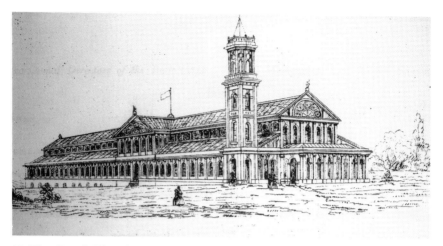

90 The Royal Victoria Park, Bath Crystal Palace, Music Hall and Winter Garden   The Bath Crystal Palace, designed in 1857, probably by James Wilson, was not built. Clearly inspired by the success of the 1851 Crystal Palace in Hyde Park, London, the citizens of Bath sought their own cast-iron and glass building and, presumably, an Early Christian Roman basilica was thought suitable for Roman Bath.

Garden to go in the park, but whether these two designs are related is unclear.

THE ABBEY CEMETERY

The eighteenth century had seen the introduction of the landscaped park, a Picturesque yet private area from which the public were excluded – unless, of course, they contributed to the Picturesque effect. The idea of landscaped, open space in the city, as opposed to a pleasure garden such as London's Vauxhall or, in Bath, Sydney Gardens, was a nineteenth-century concept and the Royal Victoria Park was an early example. With the absence of open public spaces, particularly in London, the new garden cemeteries began to assume a dual function: initially, they were used for the burial of the dead, but more often it was as a Picturesque park that they attracted the greatest number of visitors. Traditionally burials had been done in churchyards, and later in private burial grounds or chapels as well. The first large public cemetery to be opened in England, independent of a parish church, was the Liverpool Necropolis of 1825. In 1830 the London

Cemetery Company had been formed and two years later, following the cholera epidemic of January 1832, Kensall Green Cemetery was opened. But this commercialisation led to strong criticism, particularly by J C Loudon, of the unscientific and ultimately unhealthy approach taken to burials.

John Claudius Loudon arrived in Bath in the early autumn of 1843. He had travelled up from Southampton where he had been engaged in laying out a cemetery for the Corporation and it was with a similar commission in hand, but now for the Rector of the Abbey, that he came to Bath. We read, in Jane Loudon's memoir of her husband, of the extraordinary energy and persistence of this Scotsman:

> On our arrival at Southampton, where he was laying out a cemetery, he felt better; and, taking a lodging there, he sent Angus and myself back to town. In a fortnight I went down to see him, and I shall never forget the change I found in him. The first look told me he was dying. His energy of mind had now returned. He not only attended to the laying out of the cemetery at Southampton; but during his stay in that town he corrected the proofs of the second *Supplement* to his *Encyclopedia of Architecture*, and then went alone to Bath, in spite of my earnest entreaties to be permitted to accompany him.

Loudon approached cemetery design with as much energy as he did his many other interests. His thoughts on cemetery design were first published in *The Gardener's Magazine* in 1843 as a series of articles entitled *The Principles of Landscape-Gardening and of Landscape-Architecture Applied to the Laying Out of Public Cemeteries and the Improvement of Churchyards: Including Observations on the Working and General Management of Cemeteries and Burial Grounds*. These articles were collated and published later that year as a book, *On the Laying Out, Planning and Managing of Cemeteries, and on the Improvement of Churchyards*. It was at just this time that he was engaged in laying out the three cemeteries that are, in fact, the extent of his work in this field. It was both as a justification of his own designs and an appeal for a more scientific and hygienic approach to cemetery design and management that he published the articles and then the book.

The three cemeteries were laid out at Cambridge, Southampton and at Bath, in that order. It is those at Cambridge and Bath that are

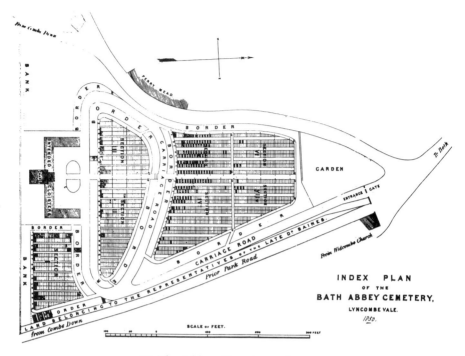

91 The Abbey Cemetery, plan

still most representative of his work: various later changes at
Southampton have made his influence imperceptible. Thus the
remaining two cemeteries are all the more important, the first as
the propagator of the ideas whose expression can be found in *The
Layout Out, Planting and Managing of Cemeteries*, and the last, the
most complete, as the culmination of the experiment.

The setting of the Abbey Cemetery [91] is remarkable, even by
Bath standards. The cemetery lies to the west of Prior Park Road
about where it becomes Ralph Allen Drive, in the fork formed at
the junction with Perrymead. The site is more or less triangular
and falls from high ground along the south edge to its lowest point
at its northern apex. In many ways it answers the criteria that
Loudon set for the perfect urban cemetery, even though its
northern aspect would reduce its exposure to sunlight:

> Cemeteries, as at present used, ought to be in an elevated and
> airy situation, open to the north, but with a south aspect, that
> the surface may be dried in the sun. . . It should be as near the
> great mass of the population for which it is intended, as a due

regard to their health will permit, in order to lessen the expense of carriage, and shorten the time of performance of funerals and of visits by the living to tombs of their friends; it ought to be conspicuous at a distance, from its buildings and tombs, it will generally be an ornament to the surrounding country, and an impressive memento to our mortality.

The principle on which the cemetery was laid out was one of division and subdivision by use of roads, walks and paths. As Loudon explained:

> There ought to be at least one main road . . . and from this road there ought to be gravel walks into the interior of the compartments formed by the roads, walks, and the boundary wall; and, from these gravel paths, ramifications of narrow grass paths, so as to admit of examining the graves.

For reasons of security there was to be one main entrance, from which would run the main road. This was the principle applied at Bath.

92 J Buckler, *The Abbey Cemetery Chapel* [91–92] Laid out in 1843, the scientifically-arranged Abbey Cemetery is the best surviving example of the three cemeteries designed by John Claudius Loudon. The Chapel, shown in Buckler's watercolour of 1847, was built by George Phillips Manners in 1843–44 and behind it can be seen the railings erected around William Beckford's tomb by H E Goodridge in 1844, and subsequently moved to the Lansdown Cemetery some four years later. See [190].

> In laying out the interior of the cemetery, the first object
> [should be] to obtain a carriage-road down the centre; not
> only for general purposes, such as cartage for materials for
> building tombs, brick graves, &, but to allow of the hearse
> approaching the graves as near as possible.

The carriage road divided the cemetery along an east-west axis. It
was further subdivided by a walkway or central avenue, broken at
one place by steps, and running downhill, south to north, from G P
Manner's Norman chapel at the top of the site [92]. At that time it
was common practice to divide cemeteries into 'imaginary
squares or parallelograms' for the easier location of plots. Yet this
was not Loudon's intention.

> It must be confessed, however, that this system of laying out a
> cemetery into imaginary squares is a very unsatisfactory
> one. . . A much better system, in our opinion, is to lay out the
> ground in what may be called double beds with green paths
> between . . . which has an orderly appearance, admits of a
> permanent system of surface drainage, requires no mapping,
> and enables the friends of the deceased to recognise the grave
> they wish to see without troubling the sexton or anyone else.

Thus each double bed took two graves head-on to each other, the
headstones placed back-to-back on a raised, two foot strip, down
the centre.
    Such uniformity of layout could be thought to provide an
unnecessarily formal appearance. Yet this was not Loudon's
intention: he merely wished to provide a memorial to the dead
more fitting than a pleasure garden.

> The layout of the ground in double beds need not be so
> executed as to have a formal appearance, though it should be
> sufficiently distinct to give what, in the language of art, is
> called the expression of purpose, and thus give the lawn of a
> cemetery a different character from that of a lawn of a
> pleasure-ground.

It seemed to matter little to Loudon that the Bath site was quite
steeply sloping. 'An uneven surface', he wrote, 'may be thrown
into beds and borders for graves on the same general principles as
in a cemetery having a flat surface'. The slope would doubtless

have served to help the land drainage which was of great importance to Loudon. 'Under every green path there may be a drain, which will render it as dry as a gravel walk.'

The other feature, apart from the layout, which survives so well at Bath is the planting. One hundred and forty-five years is a long time for a landscape scheme to survive quite intact, yet enough remains at Bath for Loudon's general principles of cemetery planting to be easily understood. Furthermore, Loudon's scheme was for relatively sparse afforestation and he was very clear as to exactly how the planting should be managed:

> On the introduction of *trees and shrubs* into cemeteries very much of the ornamental effect is dependent; but too many trees and shrubs impedes the free circulation of the air and the drying effect of the sun, and therefore they ought to be introduced in moderation. They ought not, as we think, to be introduced in masses in the interior of the cemetery, nor in strips or belts round its margin, unless under very particular circumstances. Every mode of introducing trees and shrubs which is identical with that practiced in planting parks and pleasure-grounds is to be avoided, as tending to confound the character and expression of scenes which are, or ought to be, essentially distinct. . . Almost all kinds of trees should be ever-green and of dark foliage; because the variety produced by deciduous and flowering trees is not favourable to the expression either of solemnity or grandeur.

The planting at Bath was, indeed, largely evergreen. Four yew trees remain at the junction of the central avenue and the carriage road. More yew trees mark the border alongside the access road. Other evergreens remain, yet their positioning is somewhat vague and their effect is lost. The locating of the trees, as can be discerned at Bath, was very much in the manner he had shown on his published plan for the Cambridge cemetery.

> Along each side of most or all of the main roads, whether straight or curved, we would plant a row of trees parallel to the road, and at regular distances, so as to form a running foreground to the interior of the compartments, and to whatever there might be of distant scenery. . . Along the centre of the beds adapted for double rows of graves we would plant trees or shrubs at regular distances with the

intention that . . . the trees should be taken up and replaced altogether, when necessary, so as to suit the position of graves.

This system of removing trees and shrubs once planted around the graves would probably account, together with natural turnover, for the relatively sparse planting within the boundaries. The cemetery is now quite full, and brambles, nettles and rose-bay willow-herb account for much of the planting. There is little evidence of flowerbeds and, although Loudon had published arrangements for gravel paths and flowerbeds, their non-appearance would have been to his liking, and indeed might have been his desire.

> For our own particular taste, we would have no flowers at all, nor any portion of ground within a cemetery that had the appearance of being dug or otherwise moved for the purpose of cultivation. A state of quiet and repose is an important ingredient in the passive sublime; and moving the soil for the purpose of culture, even over a grave, is destructive of repose.

Loudon further remained in Bath only to inspect some land belonging to a Mr Pinder. The *Bath Directory* for 1842 shows William M Pinder as living at Cranhill Villa, Weston Road and four years later at Brookfield, Weston Road. On his return to London designs were drawn up but whether they were implemented one cannot tell. The gardens of both houses have long since fallen victim to suburban developers. Loudon died in December 1843 and was buried in Kensal Green Cemetery, London. It is unlikely that he would have found his resting place, a pleasure-ground and catacombed, quite to his liking. His own Abbey Cemetery was consecrated by the Bishop of Salisbury on 30 January 1844 and later that same year it received, despite instructions to the contrary, the remains of William Beckford.

THE ITALIAN VILLA STYLE

In his *Encyclopedia of Cottage, Farm and Villa Architecture* J C Loudon wrote in 1833 of the Villa style:

> It is not a style which can be trusted in the hands of any Architect not a master in the art of composition . . . Italian

Architecture . . . is characterised by irregularity, by strong contrasts, and by painter-like effects. The whole, which is the result of this style, is of a more refined kind; it is addressed to a more highly cultivated taste; and to produce it requires a much higher degree of talent, than to compose in any species of regular Architecture. No architect, therefore ought to attempt the Italian style, who has not studied the composition of landscape scenery generally.

In both his *Encyclopedia* and his *Gardeners Magazine*, which ran from 1826 to 1842, as well as in other of his publications, Loudon popularized the Italian Villa style as first attempted by one man: Thomas Hope. As a pamphleteer in support of Wilkins' Greek designs for Downing College, Cambridge, Hope has already been introduced. Yet within twenty years he had rejected the necessity of creating an archaeologically sound arcadia, and had turned to the very roots of the Picturesque, the vernacular architecture of the north Italian plains. With his architect, William Atkinson, Hope turned his Palladian country house of The Deepdene near Dorking, Surrey [93] into what Loudon was to describe as 'one of the finest examples in England of an Italian villa, united with the grounds by architectural appendages.' Loudon's comment should not be misunderstood: he did not see The Deepdene as simply an Italian Villa placed in the English landscape – for it was not that – but more of an evocation of the themes expressed in north Italian rural architecture and a demonstration of their relationship to the *campagna*. Indeed to begin with the style was relatively simple and unadorned, and was thus much more representative of specifically Tuscan architecture: later it became heavy and elaborate, and more generously Italianate in expression.

The work at The Deepdene, carried out in two stages between 1818 and 1819 and in 1823, produced an irregular synthesis not only of height, shape and form, but of style and texture as well. In the first analytical work on this theme, *The Picturesque* (1927), Christopher Hussey alighted upon just this synthesis. 'Picturesque architecture' he wrote, 'is not, except in rare instances, a style but a method of using and combining styles.' The creation of the Picturesque within the buttressed and battlemented vocabulary of the Gothic was, as William Beckford had found with James Wyatt's designs for Fonthill Abbey (1796), relatively simple. At Lansdown Tower he and his new architect had to rely far more on the techniques so recently demonstrated by Hope at The Deepdene.

93 The Deepdene, Dorking, Surrey

Beckford knew Hope well: socially and culturally they had much in common and Hope, in his pursuit of Beckford's younger daughter, had visited Fonthill many times. In the event Susan Beckford married her cousin, the Marquess of Douglas and Clydesdale, the next and tenth Duke of Hamilton, a far better catch than even the wealthy Thomas Hope. Thus a real connection between The Deepdene and Lansdown Tower would appear probable, though it would seem that there was a little rivalry, on Beckford's part at least. Even in the early 1820s he is still seen gloating over possessions which Hope lacked: he had secured a better marriage for his daughter – Hope only got the daughter of the Archbishop of Tuam – and now he was to create, in his Tower, a more striking Picturesque composition than ever Hope had envisaged.

94 *An Artist's Villa*

95 'Watch towers common on smaller villas and farm houses in several parts of Tuscany'
[93–95] Copy books, such as John Claudius Loudon's *Encyclopedia of Cottage, Farm and Villa Architecture,* and John Buonarotti Papworth's *Rural Residences* served to popularize the stylistic variety of Picturesque architecture and the romance of the Italian *campagna.* Thomas Hope's house, the Deepdene, rebuilt between 1818 and 1823, was, according to Loudon, 'one of the finest examples in England of an Italian villa united with the grounds by architectural appendages'.

As an element of the emergent Picturesque, towers, so often found in Claude's paintings, had played an important role. They were used with effect at Downton Castle, Fonthill Abbey and in 1802 by John Nash at Cronkhill near Shrewsbury, Shropshire. Here, for the first time, the architectural style moved from the Gothic or the castellated to something more Mediterranean, and the over-hanging eaves, the round headed windows and the open loggias of the Tuscan villa can be recognised. Such features appeared in three separate books published in 1805: *The Rural Architect* and *Designs for Cottages, Cottage Farms and Other Rural Buildings,* by J M Gandy and *Architectural Sketches for Cottages, Rural Dwellings and Villas* by Robert Lugar. More such illustrations appeared in 1818, the same year as work began at The Deepdene, when J B Papworth published *Rural Residences,* but it was not until the second edition of 1832 that he included his prototypical 'Artist's Villa' [94], a combination of Tuscan villa architecture and Greek detailing set in a verdant, rolling landscape. The rustic, open-topped, Tuscan *campanile* of this illustration was of the type used by Hope at The Deepdene and later illustrated by Loudon in his *Encyclopedia* as 'watch towers common on smaller villas and farm houses in several parts of Tuscany' [95]. But by now, 1832, Goodridge had built the Lansdown Tower, Robert Wetten had published *Designs for Villas in the Italian Style of Architecture* (1830), Benjamin Disraeli had written *Contarini Fleming* (1832) and Thomas Hope was dead. Ironically, it might have been Hope and

The Deepdene of whom Disraeli was writing when he had his hero declare:

> I have resolved to create a Paradise . . . a Palladian Pile built upon a stately terrace . . . to which you ascend by a broad flight of steps. . . The formation of the surrounding country-side is highly picturesque, hills beautifully peaked or undulating and richly wooded. . . I have already commenced the foundation of a Tower which shall rise at least 150 feet. This Tower I shall dedicate to the Future and inside that shall be my tomb. Here let me pass my life in the study and creation of the Beautiful.

Following on from Lansdown Tower Goodridge took the Tuscan villa and the Picturesque to the far slopes of Bathwick Hill. The images and aspirations of The Deepdene were now becoming well known. J P Neale and included Hope's house in his 1826 *Views of Seats* and then published it separately, the same year, as *Account of The Deepdene*. Loudon, as we have seen, was to publish The Deepdene in 1829 and in 1833.

By this date, a quarter of the way into the nineteenth century, Bath was recognised by those who cared – such as the Tilneys and Catherine Moreland – to lack any true Picturesque qualities and was seen more in terms of regular architectural forms relating little to the treeless landscape. The terraces and villas being built at this time on the lower slopes of Bathwick Hill seemed to do little for the Picturesque: 9 Bathwick Hill [96], a neat octagonal building called Spa Villa built by John Pinch in 1820, was possibly inspired by the Tower of the Winds, but hardly Picturesque; Pinch's Raby Place [11], built slightly lower down in 1825, is far too regular even to be considered. Thus when in 1828 Goodridge began to build for himself a villa half way up the hill, called, appropriately, Montebello [97], he introduced a new theme into the domestic architecture of Bath. He followed this, many years later, with another, Fiesole, and a semi-detached pair, La Casetta and Casa Bianca. It can be understood how Walter Savage Landor, the writer and Italophile, who left his home in Fiesole and settled in Bath in 1838, came to see the city as England's Florence.

Montebello is noticeable for its steeply sloping site, its quite irregular outline of towers and chimneys and the manner in which it appears almost to overhang the road. A tall *campanile* at the back of the site towers over the building and this is balanced by a smaller, octagonal tower, now missing its upper stage, above the

96 Spa Villa, 9 Bathwick Hill

97 Montebello, Bathwick Hill [96–97] When buildings like Spa Villa and Raby Place [11], built by John Pinch in 1820 and 1825 respectively, began to appear on the hillsides surrounding Bath, they showed little response to the Picturesque possibilities of the situation. The contrast offered by H E Goodridge's Montebello, built a little higher up Bathwick Hill in 1828, is extreme.

98 Fiesole, Bathwick Hill

99 La Casetta and Casa Bianca, Bathwick Hill [98–99] By the time H E Goodridge built Fiesole and the semi-detached La Casetta and Casa Bianca on his own land on Bathwick Hill in 1848, the stylistic variety of the Picturesque and the simple austerity of the Tuscan style had given way to the more consistent, elaborate and generous Italian Villa style.

road. Although this element is suggestive of the Tower of the Winds, it is more likely to be derived from ideas contained in J G Jackson's 1828 *Designs for Villas*. The entrance façade, approached past an introductory gate lodge and up a steep curving drive, is dominated by a three-bay, double-height loggia. Between this and the tall *campanile* once stood a large conservatory decorated with Greek details. Goodridge reputedly built this imposing house to accommodate his own growing collection of books and works of art, many of which he had acquired from William Beckford: it was perhaps with collecting, as well as sketching, in mind that he travelled to Italy in 1829. Whatever else he brought back, he returned with the idea of the *campanile*, for that part of the building postdated his Italian tour.

Slightly lower down the hill, but still on his own land, he built Fiesole [98], La Casetta and Casa Bianca [99] in 1848. In that year he sold Montebello, perhaps with its contents, to the collector G H Sims, and moved to Fiesole. But now, twenty years on, these villas have departed from the Picturesque, as Hussey defined it, for no longer is the mixture of style really apparent. Furthermore, the simplicity of the Tuscan villa has been exchanged for something more elaborately Italianate. There is almost a sense of bombast in the richness of form which these buildings display. Their details, and particularly the double-height, open loggia at Fiesole, related closely to Goodridge's unrealised scheme for Lansdown Tower [100] which, following Beckford's death in 1844 and the Tower's eventual change of use to a beer garden in 1847, might be dated to these years. Goodridge had proposed the rebuilding of the simple, Tuscan architecture of the base of the Tower, in a rich Italianate manner, incorporating double- and triple-storey loggias, with chimneys and belfry, banding and blocking course.

As the style became popular, Italianate villas started to multiply on the hills around Bath. Smallcombe Grove [101], possibly by Goodridge and extended in the Greek manner by W B Gingell, has already been mentioned. Despite the Soanesque ceiling inside, the exterior, with the sweeping eaves and triumphally arched chimneys, is quite Italianate. The house was built for Benjamin Barker, the younger brother of Thomas Barker of the Doric House. He was also a landscape painter and was known as the English Poussin, an aphorism he clearly decided to live up to. The Bath architect James Wilson also chose a more Italianate expression for his own house, Glenavon [102], at the top of Sion Road on Lansdown. Here he used another octagonal tower and details

100 The Lansdown Tower, proposed alterations   In c1848 H E Goodridge
returned to the Lansdown Tower to draw up proposals for the extension of the
building in the Italian Villa style: these designs were never realised.

101 Smallcombe Lodge, Bathwick Hill   Smallcombe Lodge, now Oakwood, was built in the Italian Villa style, probably by H E Goodridge, for Benjamin Barker, a landscape painter known as 'the English Poussin'. Later additions, in the Greek manner, were by William Bruce Gingell. See [73].

102 Glen Avon, Sion Road

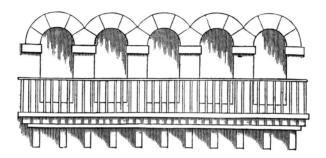

103 'A row of circular headed windows with a balcony'
[102–103] The Italian Villa style, like other informal styles, was open to interpretation. In the design of his own house, Glen Avon, James Wilson came noticeably closer to the images provided in John Claudius Loudon's *Encyclopedia of Cottage, Farm and Villa Architecture* than H E Goodridge ever did.

closer to Loudon than Goodridge ever did. The round headed windows recall that author's enthusiasm [103]:

> A row of circular headed windows, with a balcony . . . forms one of the most striking features in the elevations of Italian villas.

Following the death of Thomas Hope in 1831, his elder son Henry carried out fairly extensive alterations to the exterior of The Deepdene: these were noted by Loudon in the *Gardeners Magazine* of 1836. Yet what Henry Hope effected at The Deepdene, by 1840, was the recreation of a splendid High Renaissance Italian *palazzo*. As a demonstration of the development of the Villa style into the Palazzo style, The Deepdene is significant, but the real value of this later work is in its adaptation to a rural setting of the strongly urban forms of the Italian *palazzo*.

CHAPTER 5

Gothic Architecture

GOTHIC SURVIVAL AND THE GOTHICK

The development of Gothic architecture and church design resulting from archaeological exploration and religious revivalism, went hand in hand during the nineteenth century. As such, they have dominated much of the appreciation of nineteenth-century architecture. Yet it would be as wrong to say that all nineteenth-century churches were Gothic as it would be to say that Gothic was a nineteenth-century style. A number of Neo-Classical nineteenth-century churches have already been examined. It is the intention here to consider how mediaeval architecture was revived, even into the present century, and to understand the effect the High Church movements had on the Gothic style.

Mediaeval building methods in Britain never died after the middle ages. Although submerged for years beneath the weight of the Renaissance, they contrived to be employed as the structural basis of many buildings, such as St Paul's Cathedral, London (c1675). Occasionally they would surface as a stylistic assertion: Sir Christopher Wren's Tom Tower at Christ Church, Oxford, (1681) and Sir John Vanbrugh's Vanbrugh Castle at Greenwich (1717) attempt to look mediaeval. Only twenty-four years after Lord Burlington introduced Palladian architecture at Chiswick Villa, Horace Walpole started building his own mediaeval plaything lower down the Thames at Strawberry Hill (1749). At much the same time Ralph Allen's clerk of works, Richard Jones, had built what R E M Peach was later to describe as 'a small, but very pretty cottage' for Dodsley, the estate gardener at Prior Park, and in 1745 a temple or oratory which bore quite a resemblance to William

104 Temple from Prior Park, now at Rainbow Wood House Originally located in the grounds of Prior Park, this small temple, built by Richard Jones in 1745, is one of the very earliest examples of the Gothick in the country.

Kent's newly completed choir screen at Gloucester Cathedral (1742). This temple [104], which was moved to nearby Rainbow Wood House in 1921, had an arcade of three bays with ogee arches and thin, fanciful details but, at least externally, lacked the richness of decoration and frail expression afforded to Kent's screen. Internally, however, the walls were covered with elaborate, polygonal panels in stone ribbing. A similar arcade, but made up of more open-work, can be seen wrapping around three sides of a house on Perrymead, just across Ralph Allen Drive from Prior Park. This building, now called eponymously The Cloister, was built c1740 – which might indicate that this arcade was part of the original conception – and later extended, probably soon after 1847, when it was put up for auction, by G P Manners.

But these buildings at Prior Park, which were to include a lodge with quatrefoils and crenellations, traceried windows and a round tower (which was later partly demolished to be rebuilt as a monument to Allen himself and eventually taken down in 1953), were really more garden ornaments – albeit functional ones – than public architectural statements: the house did that effectively enough. A much more public building in the mediaeval manner was to be the chapel and minister's house built in the Vineyards for the Countess of Huntingdon's Connexion in 1765. This was much admired by Horace Walpole and, presumably, other London *literati*: after all, Alexander Pope spent months at Prior Park and was largely instrumental in the formation of parts of that landscape.

Yet this eighteenth-century architecture which tried to look mediaeval appeared thin, lacking in archaeological authority, and altogether a style *appliqué*. To distinguish it from the more correct efforts of the nineteenth-century Gothic Revival, it is often referred to as *Gothick*, using the contemporary spelling. Much as Greek and Roman architecture was being popularised in the pattern books of the time, Gothick too had its publicists. Foremost amongst these was Batty Langley, a Classicist, who sought to provide a Vitruvian analysis bedecked in Gothick parts based on either his own observations or borrowed from those of others. In *Gothic Architecture* (1747) he provided Gothick versions of the five Classical Orders with a number of alternative entablatures for each. There is also a series of doorways or frontispieces which are slightly more convincing. Yet his 'Gothick Window for a Pavillion' [105] is no more than a three-light Vitruvian or Palladian window done up with pointed arches. The influence of such fashions can be seen at the rear of no. 11 The Circus in Bath [106]: the Woods' openness to the Gothick, by way of the Castle style, has already been noted.

Behind Brock Street, between Margaret's Buildings and Church Street, the younger Wood built Margaret's Chapel in 1773. Although largely hidden from sight it was a Gothick concoction whose presence was boldly announced by a Gothick archway set amid the Classical regularity of the north side of Brock Street. The Chapel, bombed during the Second World War, has been cleared away and some correcting hand has removed the apparently unsuitable pointed arch. Yet evidence remains, for opposite, at 16 Brock Street [107], there is a tall, hooded Gothick doorway of which Batty Langley would have been proud. Other writers question its originality, but it would seem likely, considering both the narrowness of the porch and its relationship to the arched entrance opposite, that this, rather than a pedimented doorway, was the original intention. The side entrance to the chapel [108], around the corner in Margaret's Buildings, is more like what might have been expected: a pedimented doorway treated with noticeably unstructural Gothick curves. It cannot be doubted this is by Wood.

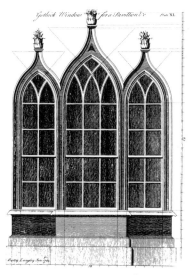

105 *Gothick Window for a Pavillion &c*, **from Batty Langley,** *Gothic Architecture, 1747*

106:11 The Circus, windows

[105–106] Batty Langley's *Gothic Architecture* contained mediaeval interpretations of familiar Palladian features. Archaeological accuracy was not a concern here, as demonstrated at the rear of No. 11 The Circus.

107 16 Brock Street, doorway

108 St Margaret's Chapel, Brock Street, doorway
[107–108] Two fanciful, Gothick doorways are the only remainders of St Margaret's Chapel which used to stand to the north of Brock Street. A Gothicised, pedimented doorway led to the Chapel from Margaret Buildings while another, less obviously Palladian, faced the chapel from 16 Brock Street.

109 All Saints' Chapel, Lansdown

Another architect of Classical crescents who employed the Gothick was John Palmer and, perhaps because it was twenty years later, he did it with somewhat more style than Wood had done before him. His most ornate Gothick building was All Saints Chapel [109] on the slopes below Lansdown Crescent, on which he was at that time engaged. Founded in 1788, but not opened until 1794, this was a large, box-like structure, heavily treated in Batty Langley Gothick. The site at the top of Park Street was prominent and overlooked the city: Palmer had not yet built St James Square below. Thus there was little need for the church to announce its presence and the small tower was used only to mark the entrance at the north (liturgical west) end of the building. The building displayed the Classical background of its architect in its rigid symmetry and formal appearance. The use of crockets and castellations was but a filigree to provide a charming and Picturesque outline. It should be noted that the stained glass and probably the altarpiece and ornaments were to the designs of Thomas Barker of the nearby Doric House. Although the Chapel was destroyed by bombing during the Second World War a few decorative details have remained, built into the house which now occupies its site.

Palmer's second church, Christ Church, Montpelier Row [110], was built in 1798. Founded in 1795 for the use of the poor, this

110 Christ Church, Montpellier Row

[109–110] Although both frail and box-like in conception, the more apparent differences between All Saints' Chapel, Lansdown, and Christ Church, Montpellier Row, built by John Palmer in 1788 and 1798 respectively, indicate the move away from Gothick finery to a more convincing mediaevalism. The illustration of Christ Church shows the battlements before they were rebuilt by Wallace Gill in c1900.

church had been funded by popular subscription and was, in fact, the first free and open church to be built in the country since the Reformation. The simplicity of its design and detailing, reflecting its charitable status, renders it noticeably different to All Saints, Lansdown. Although its arrangement was similar, a box-like hall with a small west tower flanked by lobbies, it lacked much of the elaboration of the older church and, as a result, is more of a portent of later churches. The Gothic work, though not particularly correct in the archaeological sense, is free of the finery which gave All Saints so much of its Gothick charm. The pinnacles are spindly, the buttressing unconvincing and the battlements unnecessary. (The battlements seen today are to Wallace Gill's design of c1900.)

Liturgically, or ecclesiologically, this building was no better than All Saints: if anything, it was worse. At least at All Saints Palmer had not attempted to turn church order on its head and use quatrefoil windows, an element which should be reserved for triforium or clerestory, at the lowest level of the side walls. The reason behind this was simple enough. Christ Church was a galleried church: the poor had 800 places on the ground floor and the gallery space was let to provide an adequate income for the maintenance of the building. Thus there was the need to introduce the best light at the upper level. Those on the ground floor had to make do with quatrefoil windows.

THE EARLY GOTHIC REVIVAL

In the early years of the nineteenth century the population of the suburban parishes of Bath increased steadily. Bath, as a fashionable resort, had grown up quickly during the second half of the eighteenth century and the church accommodation, never substantial, was now minimal. In 1811 the population of Walcot, Bath's biggest parish, was 20,560: yet there was only room in its churches for 4,870. This problem was not peculiar to Bath for throughout the country the continual migration of the working population towards the cities had created a want of church accommodation which the abstemious years of the Napoleonic Wars had failed to satisfy.

It was the newly and extensively developed parish of Bathwick which first addressed the problem in Bath. In the wake of Baldwin and Pinch's new building works in and around Great Pulteney Street, the population of the parish of Bathwick increased by 36%

between 1801 and 1811 (from 2,727 to 3,712) and in the next decade by 8% (to 4,009). So in 1810 a committee was formed to look into the building of a new church, and a site at the bottom of Bathwick Hill was provided by the Earl of Darlington, later the Duke of Cleveland. It was decided that John Pinch should design a church to accommodate some 1,400 people and that the elegance of the design should be 'no more than commensurate with the general style and handsome appearance of other buildings in the parish.'

Although the foundation stone had been laid in September 1814, the design was not finalised until 1817 when building work began. Pinch's church was arranged in the conventional manner and as such resembled Palmer's Christ Church of some twenty years before. It should be remembered that during this hiatus Britain had suffered what the foundation stone's inscription referred to as 'the most sanguinary conflict ever recorded in the annals of History , and the downfall of Napoleon, the despot of France'. Thus it is hardly surprising that for almost twenty years no Anglican church had been built in Bath, and so for Pinch to remain within the late-eighteenth-century church-building tradition was understandable. But where St Mary's proved to be better than Christ Church was in the quality of the architecture. Those twenty years had produced a far fuller understanding of Gothic architecture and ornamentation. At just this time the first really scholarly studies of Gothic architecture were appearing: Thomas Rickman's *An Attempt to Discriminate the Styles of English Architecture from the Conquest to the Reformation* came out in 1817 and John Britton's *The Architectural Antiquities of Great Britain* (1807 ff) and *Cathedral Antiquities of England* (1814 ff) were being published during these years.

At St Mary's [111] Pinch attempted to use the Perpendicular Gothic of the Somerset churches. The feeling of airiness and spaciousness which this style, with its large windows and comparatively unimaginative tracery, imparts was suited to the preaching-box churches of the time. And it was definitely as a preaching-box that St Mary's was intended to work. Although planned with an eastward orientation towards a shallow polygonal apse containing the holy table, the church apparently worked in reverse [112]. All the seating, whether in the aisle galleries or at the east end of the nave, faced in towards an extravagant, three-decker pulpit, located just one bay down the nave from the west end. The holy table was seemingly forgotten and all attention focused on the preacher who, when addressing a

111 St Mary, Bathwick

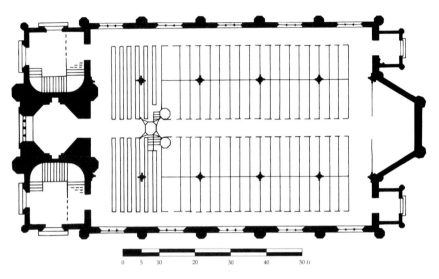

112 St Mary, Bathwick, plan

congregation from his lofty pulpit, would have stood almost eye-to-eye with those in the first row of the west end gallery. Flat and rather incorrect Gothic vaulting was applied to the ceilings of the nave and aisles, and the galleries, supported on tall thin piers of a section standard in Somerset Perpendicular churches, were decorated with repeating Gothic motifs.

Externally, the references to Somerset Perpendicular churches are easier to read, and one inevitably starts with the tower. Somerset towers, with pinnacles and battlements but without spires (with the notable exception of St Mary, Redcliffe in Bristol), are generally square on plan and can be classified, with reference to the arrangement of their upper parts, into two groups. The first group, where the tower can be regarded aesthetically as one, follow the form of Wells Cathedral. The other group, far more numerous, take the form of Bath Abbey – towers arranged in distinct, horizontal stages usually reflecting a number of different building phases. The tallest and most magnificent of this second group is St Mary Magdalen at Taunton (c1500) [113], and this is the group which Pinch sought to emulate at St Mary's, Bathwick.

Pinch's tower, buttressed at the corners, is surmounted with delicately pierced battlements and four corner pinnacles which are repeated, perhaps with reference to Bath Abbey, along the roofs of the nave and aisles. The drawings, held at the church, show that Pinch had intended to work the top of the tower in a manner

113 St Mary Magdalen, Taunton

114 St John the Baptist, Batheaston

[111–114] John Pinch's church of St Mary, Bathwick, built in 1817, was a preaching box designed to contain 1,400 people. It was encased in the traditional Perpendicular of the later Somerset churches such as St Mary Magdalen, Taunton, illustrated in John Britton's contemporary publication, *The Architectural Antiquities of Great Britain*. Earlier designs show the tower to have been based upon that at nearby St John the Baptist, Batheaston.

almost identical to that at St John the Baptist, Batheaston [114], but in the event it turned out, in its combination of lancets and quatrefoils, quite unorthodox. The treatment of the buttressing is similarly peculiar, but no more than one might expect in the early nineteenth century. Pinch does not use the angle or set back buttresses most common in the Somerset towers, but four octagonal buttresses, appearing more like corner stair turrets. His model for this could well have been the Abbey, which can be seen from St Mary's, Bathwick, but if it was then Pinch was imagining the pinnacles, which had not yet been built, and also choosing a model altogether too grand for his purpose. He would have done better to look again at St John the Baptist, Batheaston, where the single south east stair turret and its pinnacle provide a more appropriate precedent. For Pinch to use one such corner turret in a parish church would have been archaeologically acceptable; to use four was not. The decorative treatment of the tower is otherwise generally correct. The use of quatrefoil friezes to divide the stages can be found in five churches located to the east and north of Taunton: St Mary's, Huish Episcopi and its counterpart, St Martin's, Kingsbury Episcopi; St Mary's, North Petherton; St George's, Ruishton and of course, at St Mary Magdalen, Taunton. It is probably the two Episcopi churches which had the greatest influence on Pinch's overall design for the tower at St Mary's. Both towers are divided into three stages, have twin windows in the belfry and a single one in each lower stage, and measure in height 100 feet and 99 feet respectively. In arrangement, if not in detail, they correspond closely to St Mary, Bathwick and Pinch, too, made his tower 100 feet high.

Behind the tower the Somerset Perpendicular does little to hide the box-like form of the nave and aisles. Yet the large transomed four-light windows of the aisle are careful essays in the style, and precedents can be found in the aisles at St Mary's, Luccombe and All Saints', Selsworthy, near Minehead. Similar tracery appears in the tower windows, but here at St Mary's its provenance might again be attributed to the two Episcopi churches. As a church built to satisfy the growing demands of a new suburb St Mary's is really quite a fine example. This is probably because it was the product of private enterprise. The churches built with government funding to satisfy the same demand in Bath and elsewhere were rarely as accomplished.

In 1818, before St Mary's, Bathwick was finished, the first Church Building Act was passed. Through this one million pounds were made available for the Church Building Commission to remedy the deficiency of Anglican churches throughout the country. This sum, although apparently enormous, was to prove inadequate. Luckily the Commissioners managed to secure a further half million pounds through the Church Building Act of 1824 but, even so, for every church built, the parishioners had to find the greater part of the cost. The result was, inevitably, that the Church Commissioners fell well short of their target. Of the six hundred new churches they were empowered to build, they achieved only two hundred and fourteen.

The Commissioners' churches are noticeable, for the architects addressed themselves to but two problems: how to accommodate two thousand people and how, within the limited means available, to make some kind of architectural show. The result was almost inevitably a box, large and plain, with an ornate elevation, usually incorporating the tower, applied to the west end. This was exactly the form adopted by H E Goodridge at Holy Trinity, Combe Down [115]. Although built in 1835 and not a Commissioners' church, it displayed their form more effectively than the three Commissioners' churches built in Bath. Before the aisles and

115 Holy Trinity, Combe Down   In H E Goodridge's Church of the Holy Trinity, Combe Down, built in 1835, a thin and unconvincing west tower and spire hide the preaching box beyond.

chancel were added in 1884 this building was a box, bristling with pinnacles, and faced with a wild west front surmounted by an octagonal tower and spire. This façade is but a screen and the elevation has all the integrity of a Hollywood film set.

The three Commissioners' churches built in Bath were Holy Trinity, James Street; St Mark's, Lyncombe and St Saviour's, Larkhall. The first, Holy Trinity, was funded by the parliamentary grant of 1818 and the other two by that of 1824.

Holy Trinity, James Street [116] was built between 1819 and 1822 by John Lowder, who was at the same time surveyor to the city of Bath. Its function was much the same as that of Christ Church, Montpelier Row had been some twenty years earlier: to provide a free church for the poor. To this end it offered 1,810 free places and 206 in pews. The site, located on land now rebuilt between Kingsmead Square and Green Park, was awkward: it was rectangular, measuring some 100 feet by 60 feet with one long front opening onto James Street. It was the sort of site inherently suited to a Classical elevation and Lowder's first design was Greek: a hexastyle portico, one could speculate, flanked by three or four windowed bays. Lowder probably could have managed the Greek style well, for H E Goodridge had learned in his office. But this first design was thrown out by the building committee and Lowder was instructed to work in the Gothic style: the Church Commissioners thought that Gothic was the cheapest. Lowder did what he could with the site [117], running the nave along its length and marking the ends of the one elevation with a tower and spire to the east and a gable end to the west. Inside, a gallery ran the length of the north aisle and another across the west end and the ceiling was richly rib-vaulted. The elaborate, decorated east window must have been a disappointment, for it opened onto a narrow passage flanked by houses. But adequate lighting would have been provided by the clerestory windows above the south aisle. The Gothic architecture of the one elevation was thin and rather ornate, with a taste of Strawberry Hill about it. Ogee drip moulds which might have been dreamt up by Batty Langley crowned all the windows and canopied niches were set between. But all this finery was to prove, at over £14,000, too expensive and, despite a grant from the Church Commissioners of £4,000, the completed building was shorn of much of its decoration, including the canopied niches. Holy Trinity was demolished in 1957, following damage sustained during the Second World War, but the other two Commissioners' churches in Bath remain.

116 Holy Trinity, James Street

117 Holy Trinity, James Street, plan

[116–117] John Lowder built Holy Trinity, James Street, in 1819–22 as a result of the 1818 Church Building Act which made £1 million available for church building throughout the country. The Church Commissioners administered these funds and hollow edifices like this one became known as Commissioners' Churches.

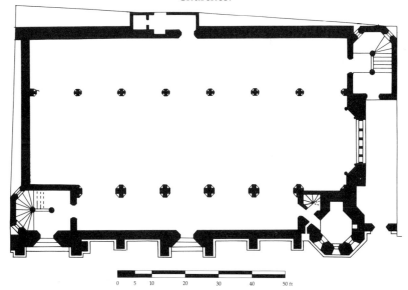

0   5   10   20   30   40   50 ft

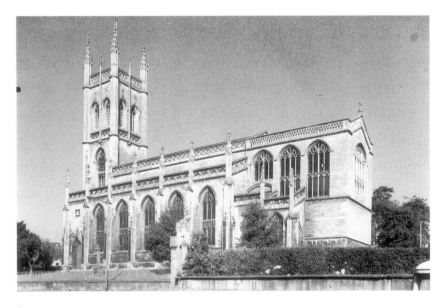

118 St Saviour, Larkhall   The second Church Building Act, passed in 1824, provided funds for the building of St Saviour, Larkhall, by the younger John Pinch, to his father's designs – compare it with St Mary, Bathwick [111] – in 1829–31. The chancel, obviously later, was added by Charles Edward Davis in 1882.

St Mark's, Lyncombe was built in 1830–1 by G P Manners, who succeeded Lowder as surveyor to the city of Bath with the new title of City Architect. It is a simple, late-Gothic building with a battlemented and pinnacled west tower, rather in the Somerset manner. Rectangular in plan, with nave and aisles (the chancel was added in 1883) it provided 631 places and 552 in pews, and cost only £10,427. St Saviour's, Larkhall [118], a much finer building, cost just £200 more. Built by the younger John Pinch to his father's designs in 1829–31, it accommodated 534 free places and 562 in pews. The arrangement took the common form of nave with galleried side aisles and west end, and a bold west tower. (Again, a chancel was added, in 1882). This church, however, owed its design to St Mary's, Bathwick and although many of the details are varied, it seems to lack much of the sparkle of the earlier essay.

It now remains to mention the last two non-archaeological Anglican churches built in Bath. And, due to their conspicuous positions, these are probably Bath's two best known churches – St Michael's, Broad Street (1835–37) and St Stephen's, Lansdown

(1840–45). Although both churches are of a rather individualistic Gothic, especially in the treatment of their west ends, they are, in a sense, transitional, when considered on plan. For here both churches move away from the preaching-box arrangement to something altogether more liturgical and of the 1840s.

This is less noticeable at St Michael's [119] where the architect, G P Manners, was very much controlled by the awkwardness of the site. Nevertheless, Manners managed a boldly vaulted church with nave and side aisles, which must originally have held galleries, as well as a south transept and a polygonal apse. Although there was no actual crossing on the plan, the transept coming out of the first bay of the south aisle, there was a structure and direction to the interior not apparent in the earlier churches.

The architectural style he used is of the twelfth- to thirteenth-century, Early English period, and this can be distinguished in the slender lancet windows and the buttresses and, inside, in the compound piers of the arcade and the pointed, quadripartite rib and panel vaulting of the roof. One of the first and most impressive examples of Early English was Wells Cathedral (c1180–1240), but the apotheosis was Salisbury Cathedral (1220–66) and as a result there are a number of fine Early English parish churches in Wiltshire. St Mary's, Wylye, for instance, might have provided the precedent, on a parish scale, for the west window. But it is more likely that the source was the east end of Salisbury itself [120], where the lancets, buttresses and corbel tables are identical to those at St Michael's. But what of the tower and spire, surely the strangest part of the west end composition? Salisbury, indeed, has a spire but there is no resemblance between it and St Michael's. A square tower breaking into an open, octagonal stage surmounted by a spire is hard to find in England: however this is largely what happens in the south west tower at Chartres Cathedral (1145–70) and, more emphatically, at Freiburg Cathedral (1310–50). Had Manners been to France or to Germany?

St Stephen's [121], built five years later by James Wilson, is no less wilful, but with its strongly expressed crossing, is very indicative of the developing trends in liturgical church design. Ironically, such a transept had not been part of the architect's original conception. Wilson had planned the church to run, without transepts, in a north-south direction much as the site necessitated. As a result the communion table was to be at the north end. But the Bishop of Bath and Wells, 'finding that the Communion Table according to the plan selected would not stand

119 St Michael, Broad Street

120 Salisbury Cathedral, east end
[119–120]Built by George Phillips Manners in 1835–37, St Michael, Broad Street, borrowed freely from Salisbury Cathedral where the lancets, buttresses and corbel tables are identical.

east and west, declared he would not consecrate such a building when completed.' As a result it was decided to build east and west transepts to accommodate the communion table and this plunged the church building committee into debt. Since no church can be consecrated until it is free of debt, it was licensed as a Chapel of Ease to Walcot in 1845 and remained thus until finally consecrated in the 1880s. Once again the architecture of the building is Early English, but now with simple tracery in the windows, suggestive

121 St Stephen, Lansdown   Built in 1840–45, James Wilson's church of St Stephen, Lansdown, remained unconsecrated for some forty years because it had been orientated the wrong way. In the meantime it had to be licensed as a Chapel of Ease to the Parish of Walcot.

of a later phase. It is the tower that dominates, and the elevated position of the building makes it all the more noticeable. The tower is in three stages, the lower one square and the upper two octagonal with big, free-standing corner pinnacles attached to the octagon by traceried, flying buttresses. This arrangement can be found in East Anglia and even in the Low Countries: consider the great castellated west tower at Ely Cathedral (c1400), or that at the more ornate St Botolph, Boston (c1510), which itself might have been inspired by the richly traceried west tower at Antwerp Cathedral (completed in 1519), or even the Cloth Hall at Bruges.

Now what these two Bath churches, St Michael's and St Stephen's, demonstrate is not so much a finer quality of architecture, but a sudden increased awareness of the importance of liturgy in church planning and of a wealth and variety of sources available, not only in English mediaeval architecture but also that of the Continent. Such an awareness was to prove to be the foundation of the High Victorian Movement in architecture.

THE HIGH-VICTORIAN GOTHIC REVIVAL

The 1830s were an extraordinary decade for the established church in England and for Gothic architecture. Reform was in the air. The first momentous occasion was the passing of the Catholic Emancipation Act in 1829. From then on the combined solidity of church and state was an anachronism: the new Whig government of 1830 was bent on parliamentary reform and, many hoped, church reform. Surprisingly, it was the short lived Tory administration of Sir Robert Peel of 1835, which, by its setting up of an Ecclesiastical Commission, largely at the instigation of Charles James Blomfield, Bishop of London, put into motion the practical church reforms which only Parliament could institute.

The prospect of such reform worried many churchmen, not so much because of the reorganisation of the church structure which it promised – this was widely accepted as necessary – but because of the apparent lack of understanding of the nature of the church as a place of God, not only amongst laymen but many clergy as well. This led to John Keble's famous sermon of 1833 in which he warned of 'National Apostasy', and the ensuing tracts of the Oxford Movement. The Tractarians, principally Keble, John Henry Newman and Edward Bouverie Pusey (all Fellows of Oriel), sought to expose and correct the general ignorance of the true nature of the church and, largely through their efforts, the Anglican church underwent a deep spiritual revival. More temporal, but only a little less so, was the effect the Anglican revival had on church architecture.

In 1839 two revivalist societies were founded at Oxford and Cambridge. The Oxford Society for Promoting the Study of Gothic Architecture, at first closely associated with the Tractarians, eventually sank from polemical prominence to become the Oxford Architectural and Historical Society. Meanwhile the Cambridge Camden Society grew, and in 1841 introduced its critical journal, *The Ecclesiologist*. In 1846, the year after J H Newman's secession in favour of Rome, they changed their name, in an attempt to appear less papish, to the Ecclesiological Society. The aim of the Cambridge Camdenians was to introduce Catholic ritual within the Anglican Church, and to monitor the upkeep, restoration and building of new churches: ecclesiology, the science of church building and decoration, was their concern. Meanwhile, quite independent of this Anglican fervour, came a prophet who was, initially, without honour. His name was Augustus Welby Northmore Pugin.

With the publication of *Contrasts* in 1836, Pugin launched his vitriolic attack on all things modern and, necessarily, pagan. The modern world was compared with the mediaeval world and came off worst every time. The fighting text of the book was accompanied, if not surpassed, by a series of sixteen plates (added to in the 1841 edition) illustrating in fine, line drawings, through comparisons or contrasts, how degenerate modern society had become. The monastery was compared with the prison or workhouse; Gothic churches were contrasted with puritan preaching boxes; and the walled mediaeval city was shown against the sprawling industrial town of the nineteenth century. In this final comparison the ragged remains of an altogether more worthy society can just be seen between the smoke-belching chimneys of the modern town. The city walks have gone and have been replaced by warehouses, the churches are in disrepair or

122 'The present state of Christian architecture'   This illustration from A W N Pugin's *Apology for the Revival of Christian Architecture*, published in 1843, offered a heroic vision of a Christian and necessarily Gothic world

123 St John the Divine, South Parade, tower incomplete

have been 'modernised', and the river clearly no longer contains fish as it once did.

The message offered by Pugin was simple [122]. The Gothic architecture of the late thirteenth century – the heroic age of Edward I (1274–1307) – was the only true architecture; and post-Renaissance Classical architecture, especially that of the present day, was abhorrent and should be rejected forthwith. *Contrasts* was a book of brilliant satire and bold in the extreme. Pugin was a Roman Catholic convert and to him Gothic architecture and Christian architecture were all one and the same. What was not Gothic was not Christian and, therefore, not suitable.

Contemporaneous with the second edition of *Contrasts* came a new assault: Pugin's *The True Principles of Pointed or Christian Architecture* was published in 1841. In this new book the message was the same, but the method was quite new. It was both appealing and witty, constructive in its criticism and demanding in its message. 'There should be no features about a building' he wrote, 'which are not necessary for convenience, construction, or propriety.'

It was no more than appropriate, therefore, that the most Puginian church remaining in Bath is the centre of Roman Catholic worship, St John the Divine [1]. The church was founded in 1861 and within two years the main body of the building and the presbytery, *sans* spire, were complete [123]. When the upper stage of the tower and the spire were eventually added in 1867 it

124 St John the Divine, South Parade Charles Francis Hansom's Roman
Catholic church of St John the Divine, South Parade, was completed, *sans* spire,
in 1863. When the spire was added in 1867, it reached to 222 feet and the church
became, for twelve years, the tallest building in Bath. The original priest's
house, shown in the illustrations, was destroyed by bombing in 1942. See [1].

reached to 222 feet and gave the Roman Catholics the tallest
building in Bath.

The architect of the church was a Roman Catholic from Bristol,
Charles Francis Hansom. Born in 1816, he was the younger brother
of J A Hansom, who is probably better remembered for the 'patent
safety cab' which bore his name. Charles Hansom was, in his time,
a leading Roman Catholic architect and on occasion he was to
receive commissions that might have otherwise gone to Pugin.
His brother, Joseph Aloysius, was at one time actually in

partnership with Pugin's son Edward Welby Pugin. Indeed Phoebe Stanton in her monograph on Pugin suggests that in 1843–44 Pugin, for the first time, found himself in competition with other Roman Catholic architects, such as J J Scoles, who were quite determined to claim their share of Roman Catholic building. Charles Hansom was one of whom he did not altogether approve. The names of Hansom and Pugin are linked, though not in partnership, in a number of buildings; church fittings and stained glass by Pugin can be seen in a few of Hansom's churches.

The exterior of St John the Divine [124] is, as *The Builder* of 1863 commented, 'one mass of gables' and, with the exception of the belfry which is really more late Early English in appearance, it is in the Decorated style of the late thirteenth and early fourteenth century. Beyond the base of the belfry a single ridgeline runs along the nave to the east, terminating in a foliated cross at the point of the apse roof. Here, at the east end of the church, the ground falls away quickly to the River Avon, giving the effect of great height to the polygonal apse. On the north side of the building six gables house the baptistry, porch, aisle and transept. The south side, however, was largely hidden by the presbytery in a more domestic Gothic style. This building was totally destroyed by bombing in the Second World War and the new presbytery, by Alec French and Partners, is an unconvincing replacement.

The interior of the church was rich [125] though, sadly, little evidence of the original colour scheme has survived bombing and redecoration. The columns of the nave arcade were of polished red Devonshire marble with capitals of Ancaster stone. The altar was of polished marble and alabaster, the work of Messrs Earp of London, and the stained glass was by John Hardman of Birmingham. The name of John Hardman and Co was to metalwork and glass what Minton was to tiles. Much of their metalwork was made to the designs of Pugin, with whom Hardman was in partnership. It was he who produced all the minutiae for the Houses of Parliament, from decorative nails to inkwells.

One of the first things one notices about St John the Divine is the use of rough-faced Bath stone. Nowhere is to be seen the smooth, machine-like quality employed, for instance, by Manners at St Michael, Broad Street. Ashlar is used only where sharp lines are needed – around openings, corners and mouldings. The rough-faced stones are small, and although evenly coursed, give the building an increased sense of scale. In *True Principles* Pugin

125 St John the Divine, South Parade, interior

stated very emphatically that *'large stones destroy proportion'*. The quoins and stones forming the door and window jambs are, however, quite regular, and this to Pugin would have smacked of modern work and been quite unacceptable. 'By this means,' he wrote, 'the effect of the window is spoiled; the eye, owing to the regularity of these projections, *is carried from the line of jamb to them*, while in the old masonry the irregular outline of the stones does not interfere with the mouldings of the window.'

There is very little about the exterior of the building that is not 'necessary for convenience, construction or propriety.' It is also true to say that all the ornament is no more than an enrichment of the essential construction of the building. For the throwing-off of rain water, the moulds are simply splayed. Strings and copings are treated in the same way, being almost so straightforward that one thinks Hansom should have heeded Pugin's warning that 'monotony should be carefully avoided, also all cutting shadows near the outer edge, which have a meagre effect.' The splays of the window and door jamb, particularly those of the west and north porches are good, the original splayed form never being lost in the sinkings of the mould.

A similar directness can be seen in the window-hood moulds, some very finely decorated, which project, as Pugin recom-

126 St John the Divine, South Parade, interior
[125–126]Architecturally thin and of muted decoration, there is little about the interior of Charles Francis Hansom's St John the Divine, South Parade, to recall A W N Pugin's Heavenly vision. The most ornate feature, the chancel screen, was a later addition.

mended, 'immediately above the springing of the arch to receive the water running down the wall over the window, and convey it off on either side. This projection' he continued, 'answers a purpose, and therefore is not only allowable but indispensable in the pointed style; but a projection down the sides of the jamb, where it would be utterly useless, is never found among the monuments of antiquity.'

It was not only for the details of buildings that Pugin set his standards. The forms and massing of the building were equally important. Towers needed spires, and pitched roofs needed to be reasonably steep. 'When towers were erected with flat embattled tops, *Christian architecture was on the decline*' and a roof that was not of the correct equilateral pitch appeared 'either painfully acute or too widely spread.'

The pinnacles that surround the tower are totally necessary, and thus warrant decoration. As Pugin said:

> At the bases of great spires, the clusters of pinnacles are also placed to increase strength and resistance; in short, wherever pinnacles are introduced to pure Pointed architecture, they will be found on examination to fulfil a useful end.

There was also a mystical interpretation for the use of the pinnacles: 'Their mystical intention is, like other vertical lines and terminations of Christian architecture, to represent an emblem of the restoration'. Furthermore, the use of high, unbroken ridgelines served to make the church more noticeable above the surrounding houses. This would mean that no chancel arch was reflected in the roof form of the building, the roof of the nave merging smoothly with that of the apse. Here Hansom defined the chancel by placing a cresting of pointed and gilded ironwork along the eastern part of the roofline.

Internally the church, as it stands today, is very muted and hardly a reflection of a Pugin interior. The construction, however, is honest. Bosses rather than pendants stud the ceiling of the chancel. As Pugin explained, 'a key-stone is *necessary* for the support of arched ribs; the older architects content themselves with enriching it with foliage or figures, but those of the later styles allowed four or five feet of *unnecessary stone to hang down into the church* and from it to branch other ribs upwards. This is at most an ingenious trick, and quite unworthy of the severity of Pointed or Christian architecture.' The timber ceilings over the nave and aisles are equally unpretentious. The spandrels of the arched timber braces spanning the nave and aisles [126] are pierced with foils and mouchettes and the space between is divided into large rectangular panels. The metalwork of the chancel and chapel screen generally reflects a *fleur-de-lis* motif but is of a later date.

It seems clear that the Puginian influence is largely expressed in the exterior of the church, yet with a few reservations. Certainly statuary, such as the figure above the door to the north porch, is placed beneath a canopy rather than mounted on pinnacles. 'Detached images surmounting buildings' as Pugin said, 'are characteristic of southern and Italian architecture, and are much better suited to the climate of Milan than that of England.' But the detail is light, the buttresses few, and the mouldings rather bland. One cannot help but feel that Pugin would have produced a finer if perhaps a thinner and more spindly church. It might be said that Hansom's architecture here is Puginian, but it lacks some of the more fanciful qualities and the fervency associated with the style of that zealous convert.

It would seem likely that it was also C F Hansom who built both of the two funerary chapels in the Perrymead Roman Catholic Cemetery [127]: he is known to have built one of them. This cemetery is located just behind and above Loudon's Abbey Cemetery and provides a considerable contrast in both arrangement and architecture. Whereas the Abbey Cemetery was rigorous in its layout and heavy in its architecture, the Perrymead Cemetery is loose and lightweight – or unscientific in layout and Decorated in architecture. The most elaborate of the two chapels, the one known to be by Hansom [128], is the Eyre family Mortuary Chapel which stands close to the gate. Small and, with a polygonal east end and unbroken ridgeline, noticeably French in arrangement, it recalls La Sainte Chapelle in Paris or Sir Gilbert Scott's Chapel at Exeter College, Oxford (1856). It is built of Bath stone, with a buttressed porch and a polygonal tower and spire placed

127 Perrymead Cemetery

picturesquely on the north side. The interior is richly marbled, with tiles by Minton and ironwork by Hardman. It was consecrated in a private ceremony presided over by Bishop Clifford of Bristol in October 1863 and it is still maintained by the family today. The other chapel, the funerary chapel for the cemetery, is less elaborate yet competent in its Decorated architecture, with a central belfry and steeply raked buttresses.

The second Roman Catholic church, Our Lady Help of Christians (St Mary's Catholic Church) [129], could here be

128 The Eyre Mortuary Chapel

[127–128] As architect of St John the Divine, it is likely that Charles Francis Hansom also built the funerary chapel at the Perrymead (Roman Catholic) Cemetery: he did build the noticeably French Eyre Mortuary Chapel there in 1863.

mentioned. It was built by Edward Joseph Hansom and Archibald Matthias Dunn in 1879–81 (of whom it was said that Dunn saw that it was handsome and Hansom saw that it was done). E J Hansom was the son of C F Hansom, in whose office Dunn had trained. Thus this church clearly represents the next generation's interpretation of church architecture and as such is noticeably post-Puginian. What is different is the scale and proportion of the church. There is less vertical emphasis and the result is a building which, externally, appears rather stretched and thin. This is probably because the building is incomplete, the west end being merely a screen wall. Had a tower, for instance, been added at this point, then the building would have been better balanced. Inside, where the sculpture is good – birds and flowers around the arch to the Lady Chapel and angels along the aisle arcade [130] – and where the marvellous reredos is of Puginian conception, the old verticality remains.

It would be wrong to think that the teachings of Pugin were reserved for Roman Catholic architects alone. Since the principles he proposed were so close to what many High Anglicans were thinking at the time he was seized upon eagerly by some, and few were more enthusiastic over Pugin than the most prolific church builder of the nineteenth century, Sir Gilbert Scott. Although he was born actually a year before Pugin in 1811, Scott was very much Pugin's disciple. On first becoming aware of Pugin's writings, Scott declared:

> Being thus morally awakened, my physical dreams followed the subject of my waking thoughts.

Scott used many of Pugin's arguments in his own *Remarks on Secular and Domestic Architecture*. It was even commented by Benjamin Ferrey in *Recollections of Pugin* that 'were Pugin now alive what a "Contrast" he might draw between the condition of Ely Cathedral in 1834 and its present state! – so beautifully has it been restored by G Scott (*a Protestant architect*).'

At the time that Hansom was building St John the Divine, Scott was engaged on the restoration of the Abbey. He was nearing the height of his career: in 1863 he had begun work on his best known work, the Albert Memorial in London. In Bath that year the parish of Walcot received a new rector and this new incumbent realised that his vast, sprawling parish of some 30,000 souls was quite inadequately served. Although there were seven places of

129 Our Lady Help of Christians (St Mary's Catholic Church), Julian Road

130 Our Lady Help of Christians (St Mary's Catholic Church), Julian Road, interior

[129–130] Built by Edward Joseph Hansom and Archibald Matthias Dunn in 1879–81, the church of Our Lady Help of Christians, Julian Road, hides a frail yet beautifully carved interior behind a rather overextended and apparently incomplete exterior.

worship, including Christ Church, Margaret Chapel and St Stephen's Chapel of Ease, only the parish church, St Swithin's on London Street, was recognised for the holding of baptisms and marriages. So it was determined to build a new church for all classes in the parish and a site behind the Royal Crescent mews, a triangle of land originally intended by the Woods for a church, was decided upon. This site was bought for £2,672 and Scott was invited to design the building.

131 St Andrew, Julian Road

132 St Andrew, Julian Road

133 St Andrew, Julian Road, plan

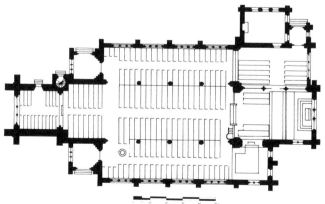

The foundation stone for the new church of St Andrew was laid amid much celebration in April 1870 and by September 1873 the building, *sans* spire, was complete. The spire was built by 1879 and, at 240 feet, was the tallest landmark in Bath [131] – thus restoring Anglican supremacy. The total cost of the works, which had been supervised by Scott's second son John Oldrid Scott, came to £24,772.18s.10d. One result of the building of St Andrew, which was to receive full parochial status, was that the younger John Wood's Margaret Chapel was closed.

St Andrew was a big church [132], seating about a thousand, and boldly expressed. It dominated the mews as much as it dominated the skyline of the Royal Crescent itself. It is worth here quoting Pevsner's stricture written in the mid-1950s:

> Big E E [Early English] tower originally with broach spire (of Rutland precedent), the rest happily bombed. The tower is now also coming down – a blessing; for it was unacceptable even from the picturesque mixer's point of view.

Built in the Early English style and devoid of unnecessary trimmings, St Andrew appeared both sturdy and plain, and it was not intimidated by its surroundings. It was in many ways typical of Scott's mature churches. The arrangement was basically symmetrical – a nave and chancel, side aisles and a centrally placed west tower [133] – and its regularity was further expressed through the use of buttresses which, in a church with a timber roof, are not strictly necessary. The decoration was minimal – nothing that was not necessary for convenience, construction or propriety – and was reserved for the pinnacles at the east end and for the tower. The very form of the broach spire, probably derived from St Peter at Rounds (or Raunds), Northampton (or, as Pevsner suggests, a nearby Rutland source), defied any decoration: compare it, for instance with the elaborate spire at St Michael, Broad Street. Internally the church was formal and ordered [134]; a clear, processional route ran from west to east with three steps, representing the Trinity, dividing the nave from the chancel and another three surrounding the altar. The east end was square and the chancel was well defined in the crucifixed roofline of the building: the arrangement was particularly English and the iconography High Anglican. Yet Scott did not always satisfy the ecclesiologists. He remained, as a businessman, really a broad-church architect, or as some said, a little ungenerously, a

134 St Andrew, Julian Road, interior [131–134] Sir Gilbert Scott's church of St Andrew, Julian Road, built in 1870–73 (the spire being added in 1879) was a rather brutal statement of Anglican supremacy. Liturgically structured both in plan and elevation, it was in every way the symbol of the established Church and nothing, it seemed, not even the Royal Crescent, was allowed to get in its way. During the Second World War it was, as Pevsner put it, 'happily bombed' and its site now remains as a triangle of well-used grass.

compromiser. As a result his churches maintained a Puginian flavour and never fully embraced High Victorian Gothic.

In Bath at this time, however, a new nave for St John the Baptist, Bathwick Street was being built, which can be seen as a far better expression of High Victorian Gothic. Its architect was Arthur Blomfield, son of that reforming Bishop of London, C J Blomfield. The original church of St John the Baptist was hardly old, it was just too small. Intended to replace the mediaeval church, it had been built in 1861–2 to the designs of a west country architect C E Giles, the tower and spire being added in 1865 [135]. Giles was a prolific church builder in the 1860s and had earlier been in partnership with Richard Carver who, in 1839, had become surveyor to the county of Somerset. It was probably in this capacity that *The Ecclesiologist*, in 1843, reckoned that Carver had 'proved himself entirely ignorant of the principles of ecclesiastic architecture'. Yet there was, as Blomfield must have recognised, nothing particularly wrong with Giles' Early English church, except for its size, which was inappropriate for a church seeking parochial status. It consisted of a nave and clearly defined chancel with a small vestry off to the north side. The tower at the north-west corner appeared barely attached to the church, in the contemporary High Victorian manner, and provided a porch. But Blomfield's additions were designed to dominate.

Between 1869 and 1871 Blomfield enlarged the church so that it could seat 600 by adding a large nave to the south side of the old building which, as a result, became the north aisle. Blomfield's design reflected much of the current thinking among leading church architects and demonstrated a very cosmopolitan approach. High Victorian Gothic was largely propagated through

135 St John the Baptist, St John's Road

Church : of : St : John : Baptist : Bath : 1861 + N : E : View : C : E : Giles : Arch^t.

136 St John the Baptist, St John's Road

[135–136] C E Giles' small church of St John the Baptist, St John's Road, built in 1861–62 (the tower added in 1865), was extended by Arthur Blomfield in 1869–71. Redolent of John Ruskin's *Lamp of Power*, Blomfield's additions overwhelmed the older building, turning it into a north aisle.

the pages of *The Ecclesiologist* and the writings of John Ruskin. Indeed, the Ecclesiological Society had sought to demonstrate their own ideas for church design when they had William Butterfield build All Saints, Margaret Street in London (1850). Ruskin, on the other hand, built nothing, but knew how to write persuasively. His most original architectural thoughts appeared in *The Seven Lamps of Architecture* (1849) which was soon followed by *The Stones of Venice* (1851 and 1853). Of the seven Lamps, the two which shone out, architecturally, were the Lamp of Truth and the Lamp of Power. In the former he followed Pugin to some extent, but his interest was more with the expression of the true nature of materials, and particularly their colour, an element he had found so impressive in his continental wanderings. The Lamp of Power was concerned with the Sublime qualities of architecture, the expression of size and simplicity of form. This was what was suggested by Giles' tower at St John the Baptist: a free standing tower in the nature of an Italian *campanile*, rising unbroken and bounded by continuous lines from ground to belfry – but at this point there is no heavy crowning cornice and the image breaks down.

Blomfield's nave is vigorous and massy [136]. Viewed from the south, from where Giles' church cannot be seen, it could never be regarded as Picturesque, which Scott's St Andrew, despite Pevsner's stricture, might have been. The windows on the south side are the simplest kinds of openings, flat French plate tracery set with bold chamfers and severe outlines. Simple tracery and buttresses alternate unbroken along this whole elevation, their strength being in their repetition, and the same strength is sensed, inside [137], in the solid arcade where Blomfield punched through the south wall of the old church to make the north aisle. Here, as in the rood screen, the architectural details were intended to be both simple and bold.

The arrangement of the building is interesting and indicative of its High Church nature. Although there is no crossing (the south transept arch is filled with the organ) the church has both a choir and a chancel. The now richly ornate rood screen, the result of work by Sir Ninian Comper in 1923, divides the nave from the choir and at this point the hammer-beam roof changes to simpler panels. Beyond the choir is the shallow chancel, so shallow that it is hardly defined. But there is a stone chancel arch and at this point the church, internally, becomes perceptibly narrower. It is here that the vigorous qualities of Blomfield's design become most apparent. The narrowness of the chancel is achieved largely by an immense thickening of the walls, so much so that the sedilia can be easily accommodated. Externally, the end-bay windows [138] are sunk between vast piers of stone which are neither really wall nor buttress. And the roof continues over the recessed windows like a heavy, frowning eyebrow.

Before leaving St John the Baptist the small baptistry at the west end of the old church should be visited. Originally built in 1879, the mosaic floor and the flat, panelled and painted ceiling suggest, again, the later hand of Comper.

It was probably indicative of his genius that Ruskin soon lost interest in the High Victorian Gothic he had helped to create. His last major architectural pronouncement appeared in his Edinburgh *Lectures on Architecture and Painting* of 1853. His place was taken, to some extent, by George Edmund Street who was somewhat more down-to-earth and wrote, not as an aesthete, but as an architect. Street had been publishing in *The Ecclesiologist* since 1850 when he wrote 'On the Proper Characteristics of a Town Church'. In this article he pointed out the necessity to avoid rusticity (the Picturesque) and to concentrate on regularity. His call for the use of clerestory lighting was heeded by Blomfield at St

137 St John the Baptist, St John's Road, interior

John the Baptist. Furthermore, Street recommended long, continuous ridgelines to take in both nave and chancel, and at St John the Baptist there is no break in the roofline where the choir and chancel join the nave, just a crucifix and a change in the style of ridge tile.

Street's recommendations in this early paper were based on his study of early French, thirteenth-century architecture [139]. Here he had found the strength and robustness which was thought

138 St John the Baptist, St John's Road, east end

[137–138] Bold lines and simple forms characterize the interior and exterior details of Arthur Blomfield's rebuilding of St John the Baptist, St John's Road. Thick walls and plate tracery, as seen in the arcade and the windows, all contribute to the vigorous quality of this design.

lacking in English architecture. Writing in the *Ecclesiologist* in 1852 on 'The True Principles of Architecture and the Possibility of Development', he observed that 'the wonderful beauty of the apsidal east ends abroad ought to be gladly seized upon'. English churches traditionally had square east ends; rounded east ends, such as Street had noticed in France, provided further means for the expression of solidity. The excitement caused by the Lille Cathedral competition of 1856 (won by William Burges and with G E Street in second place) only served to strengthen the interest in French Gothic. The ideas were taken furthest in London churches of the 1860s, John Loughborough Pearson's church of St Peter at Vauxhall (1860) [140] being perhaps the epitome of the High Victorian town church.

Although nothing of quite this scale was built in Bath, the influence was to be seen. For a change, it was not a visiting architect but a local practitioner who built in Bath in this early French style. The church of St Paul, now Holy Trinity in Monmouth Street [141], was designed by Wilson and Willcox, probably in 1869, and opened in 1874. In a way it owes a lot to Blomfield's earlier St John the Baptist – the buttressed south sides are not dissimilar – but the French allusion is taken further by the rounding off of the nave into a semi-circular apse, the chancel being indicated only by a change in the design of the windows and cornice. A more noticeable example of this is the rather later

139 Notre Dame, Paris
140 St Peter, Vauxhall, London

141 St Paul, Monmouth Street

142 St Peter, Twerton

[139–142] The unbroken rooflines and rounded east ends of French 13th century Gothic were picked up by John Loughborough Pearson at St Peter, Vauxhall, in 1860. The same French influence can be seen in James Wilson and William Willcox's St Paul, Monmouth Street of 1869 and Charles Edward Davis' St Peter, Twerton of 1876.

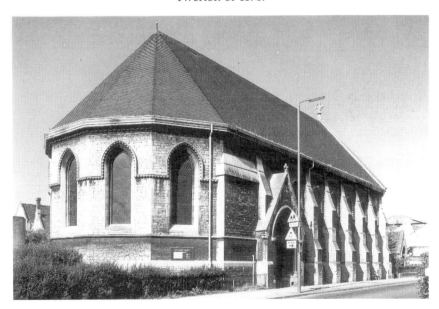

church of St Peter at Twerton [142], built between 1876 and 1880. Here C E Davis built two quite French buildings – the church and the hall – in line beside the Lower Bristol Road. In the church, the apse is polygonal rather than rounded, and the windows are free from tracery, rather in the manner of Pearson. The overall horizontal form of the church, no tower and a continuous roofline, is countered by the heavy verticality of the buttressing and the angles of the polygonal apse. (The roofline was originally pierced

143 Manvers Street Baptist Church

by a spirelet or lantern, suggestive of a French *flèche*.) The result is a strongly knit composition, simple and muscular and shamelessly early French.

144 St Paul's, Monmouth Street

[143–144] James Wilson and William Willcox built four churches in Bath with similar west fronts: Somerset Street Chapel of 1868; Hay Hill Baptist Chapel of 1869; Manvers Street Baptist Chapel of 1872; and St Paul, now Holy Trinity, Monmouth Street of 1873 (the smaller gable being added in 1880–81). Although, in their combination of French and English Gothic elements, they are stylistically varied, they are all likely to be the work of Willcox who had joined Wilson in 1866.

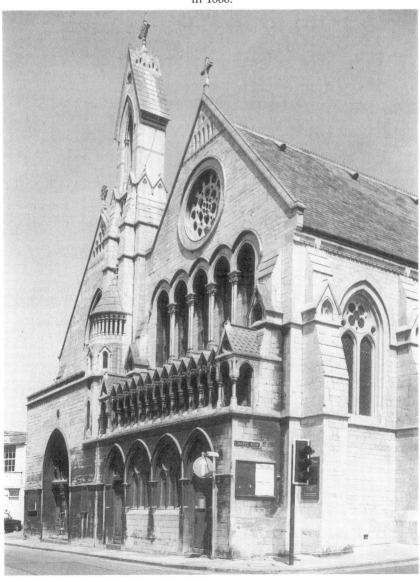

145 Gas Works, Lower Bristol Road

But to return to St Paul's. This church was one of four very similar churches designed in the late 1860s. William Willcox had joined James Wilson in 1866 and almost immediately a string of churches with similar asymmetrical west fronts emanated from the office: Somerset Street Chapel (1868), Hay Hill Baptist Chapel (1869), Manvers Street Baptist Chapel (1872), and St Paul's (1873). Although none of these other designs for west fronts are as convincing as the designs for the south side and east end of St Paul's, they are, nevertheless, interesting. The arrangement of a simple, gabled west front with a small corner tower or bellcote, as at the Manvers Street Baptist Chapel [143], recalls French models such as the Cistercian Church at Pontigny near Auxerre. At Manvers Street the French connection can actually be taken further, if the open bellcote on the tower is compared with those at Notre-Dame-la-Grande at Poitiers. And is there a hint of this in the lower stage of the belfry at St Paul's? If so, it would be out of place, for despite the early French treatment of the nave and the asymmetrical gabled arrangement of the west front, the heavy arcading of the rather awkward narthex and the row of lancets above are clearly Early English [144]. The original arrangement of this facade is, admittedly, particularly hard to appreciate: the large second gable to the left of the bellcote was added in 1880–81.

The other great Continental influence upon High Victorian Gothic was the mediaeval architectures of northern Italy – Lombardic Romanesque and Italian Gothic. Its greatest advocates, particularly in the case of the Gothic were, again, Ruskin and Street; and even Scott included a lengthy appendix on the applicability of the style in his *Remarks on Secular and Domestic Architecture* of 1858. There is, however, little evidence of the north Italian Gothic in Bath: we see it in London at Scott's St Pancras Station (1868–74) or in Bristol at Ponton and Foster's former Bristol Museum and Library on Queen's Road (1866–71) and at Ponton and Gough's Granary on Welsh Back (1871). In Bath, the evidence is largely found in details on domestic work – a brick headed

146 S Fermo Maggiore, Verona

[145–146] Lombardic architecture, as illustrated in G E Street's *Brick and Marble Architecture, Notes of a Tour in the North of Italy*, was used by George Phillips Manners and J Elkington Gill in the Gas Works, now demolished, which were built on the Lower Bristol Road in 1858.

window here, a porch there, or, until recently, in industrial buildings.

The Gas Works Office on the Upper Bristol Road, an uninspiring Italianate building, was built in 1858 by G P Manners and his young partner, J Elkington Gill. Behind this, where the city dump is now located, once stood a great red brick building with ten gabled bays [145] facing onto the river. This was Bath's most splendid expression of Lombardic Romanesque. In 1855, just three years before the Gas Works Office was built, Street published his vastly influential *Brick and Marble Architecture, Notes of a Tour in the North of Italy* which built upon foundations provided a couple of years earlier by John Ruskin's *Stones of Venice*. In his book Street illustrated both Lombardic Romanesque and more pointedly Gothic works and the influence of these great brick buildings, such as S Fermo Maggiore at Verona [146], was clearly evident along the Gas Works' river frontage. When the firm of Cotterell and Spackman rebuilt Bellott's Hospital in Beau Street the next year, 1859, the north Italian influence became apparent again, now in the polychromatic relieving arches which were inserted into the otherwise plain sandstone of the façade. Arches of just this shape, texture and colour had been illustrated in Street's *Brick and Marble Architecture*.

Whether Street, Ruskin or, indeed, Scott saw the north Italian mediaeval architecture as more suitable for Gas Works than a rebuilt hospital, would be a matter for conjecture. Perhaps Scott had buildings such as these in mind when he wrote, in 1858:

> The Gothic revivers have of late been somewhat severely taunted by their opponents, on the free use they have made of ideas derived from the Italian works of the middle ages. It is likely enough that we may be more or less deserving of such taunts, and I feel rather glad of them as curbs upon the tendency to which we are all liable, to depart from the strictness of our own principles and to indulge in too free an eclecticism.

The only ecclesiastical example of north Italian Gothic in Bath was, in fact, by Scott – the Chapel at Partis College [147]. In 1862, soon after he was appointed architect to the Abbey, he completely reworked the small chapel hidden behind the college's imposing portico. Taking the centre line of the portico as his axis, he turned the chapel round through ninety degrees and built a new, rounded

147 Partis College Chapel, interior Sir Gilbert Scott introduced constructional polychromy to the interior of the chapel he added to Partis College in 1862. 'Alternating voussoirs of stone and brick', he wrote of Italian architecture, 'are exceedingly beautiful'.

apse on what was the northern side. The small nave was divided from the even smaller aisles by a three bay arcade whose rounded voussoirs were of alternating red and white stone, the effect being similar to that already noted at Bellott's Hospital. The same noticeably Italian treatment was employed over the chancel arch in combination with stiff-leaf capitals. In his comment on 'The Uses to be Made of the Mediaeval Architecture of Italy' he recommended such polychromatic construction:

> The form, perhaps, of constructive polychromy which most concerns ourselves is that produced by the use of brick and

148 St Mary, Bathwick, chancel

stone (with occasional addition of marble). Verona is
peculiarly rich in work of this kind. In these works we usually
find each order of the arches of doorways, windows, &c., in
alternating voussoirs of stone and brick . . . these features are
exceedingly beautiful.

The same effect can be noticed in the arcades at St Andrew, Julian
Road.

After so much talk of French and Italian work it might be
expected that G E Street's one building in Bath would be a rich
expression of High Victorian Gothic. Sadly it is not so. This was
the new chancel built at St Mary, Bathwick [148], between 1871 and
1873, and Street's designs had been chosen in preference to those
of the Bath man, J Elkington Gill. It must have been something of
an achievement to have Mr Street build the chancel. Street's
practice at this time was very busy. As well as being one of the
leading church builders – he was taking on about eight new
churches a year – he also was engaged in the complex building of
the Law Courts in London. In 1868, the same year as he eventually
received the Law Courts commission, Street had begun work on
both Bristol Cathedral and All Saints, Clifton and since visits to
Bristol must have been frequent, it would have troubled him little
to alight from the train at Bath.

Lack of space precluded a large addition and the new chancel was only 35 feet long, yet onto the site Street worked a narrow Lady Chapel, sacristy and other rooms. The Gothic he used was far more correct than Pinch's, and of the early fourteenth-century Decorated period. The east window combines the flowing, ogival forms of curvilinear tracery with the simpler, symmetrical forms of geometrical tracery. A similar combination can be seen in the windows of Wells Chapter House (c1310). The whole interior of the chancel [149] was richly decorated to Street's specification – glass, paintwork, metalwork and furnishings. The glass was designed and manufactured by the leading decorators, Clayton and Bell (who, incidentally, did the mosaics on Scott's Albert Memorial) and they too applied the stencilled paintwork, although this has since gone. The metalwork, most evident in the low chancel screen and the pulpit, was manufactured by Singers of Frome and, in its tendril forms, is very reminiscent of the Italian and Spanish mediaeval ironwork Street so admired.

149 St Mary, Bathwick, interior

[148–149] In 1871–73 George Edmund Street added a three-bay chancel in the Decorated style of the early 14th century to St Mary, Bathwick. Although archaeologically correct, it is somewhat at odds with John Pinch's use of the Perpendicular elsewhere, but it did have the effect of reordering the interior of the church. Here the new pulpit is carved by Thomas Earp and the chancel screen is by Messrs Singers of Frome.

The chancel at St Mary represents not so much a bold example of High Victorian Gothic – it is not that – but a carefully considered and thoroughly thought out church rebuilding commission from one of the country's leading church architects. Street's total scheme for the east end of this early nineteenth-century church only makes up in thoroughness what it lacks in compatibility. The impression it leaves, particularly inside, is of the chancel of one church fused to the nave of another and the regret is that Street's brief did not, apparently, include the rest of the church: maybe this was because the funds only reached to £3,000. There must have been a strong case, in 1871, for reworking an inconvenient church barely fifty years old. The ice, however, was that much thinner when it came to reworking the Abbey.

BATH ABBEY AND THE PROBLEM OF RESTORATION

In 1860 Sir Gilbert Scott had been called in to look at the Abbey. The building with which he was confronted was in a sad state of repair so he proposed a three phase scheme for the Abbey's restoration:

1. The repair of the roof and clerestory with the East, West and large transept windows.
2. The repair of the remaining windows and the groining of the nave and aisle ceilings.
3. The repair of the lower parts of the building, the removal of the galleries, the rearrangement of the seats and provision of improved means of lighting, heating and ventilation.

The estimate for this work, which was eventually approved on 30 April 1864, was in excess of £20,000. In the event, Scott's restoration was carried out more or less as proposed [150]. Annual reports were published by the Bath Abbey Church Restoration Committee between 1865 and 1872 and these provide an adequate guide as to how work progressed. Much of the restoration of the west end was done *gratis* by the Freemasons of Somerset and almost finished by 1867. At that time the stone groining of the transept had been completed as had three-fifths of the ceiling of the nave and the nave aisles. The roof and battlements of the south

150 Bath Abbey   The west front of Bath Abbey as it appeared in c1895 – after George Phillips Manners and Sir Gilbert Scott had done their restoration but before Sir Thomas Graham Jackson did his.

transept, which had been left out of the initial contract, were attended to at this stage. By the next year the organ had been built in the north transept and at the end of 1869 *The Bath Chronicle* could report that 'about two thirds of the entire work had been done'.

During 1869 Edward Blore's stone screen of 1835, above which the organ had been located, was taken down and repositioned at the west end of the nave to form an inner porch. Work now started on the lighting of the building, the tender of £1,100 by Messrs Skidmore of Coventry being accepted. By 1870, thirteen stained glass windows had been installed, that at the east end being by Messrs Clayton and Bell. The *Report* of 1872 anticipated the restoration coming to an end in the spring of the following year, with the exception of some fittings such as stalls and the pulpit,

151 Bath Abbey, interior   The choir of Bath Abbey, photographed in 1875 following Sir Gilbert Scott's restoration, showing the new gas chandeliers which he added and the old fan vaulting which he extended down the nave.

the latter to be built to Scott's design at a later stage [151].

It would seem that by 1872 the Bath Abbey Church Restoration Committee could be well pleased with the work which Scott had done for them but the fact was that at Bath, as well as at many other greater and lesser churches, Scott and other mid-century church restorers were fueling a problem which was soon to give vent to a fearful rage. For it was only three years later that William Morris wrote to *The Athenaeum*, taking Scott to task for his proposed 'restoration' of Tewkesbury Abbey and calling for the setting up of 'an association for the purpose of watching over and protecting these relics, which scanty as they are, are still wonderful treasures'. The result was the foundation, in 1877, of the Society for the Protection of Ancient Buildings.

On the surface Scott might appear no more dastardly in his restoration work than any leading architect, yet his recommendations could, at times, be extreme. After his first visit to the Abbey in 1860 he had written to the Rector saying:

> What I suggest, then, is the removal of the screen which separates the nave from the choir, and a general rearrangement of the whole and entire church.

And it was just such attitudes which so infuriated the members of SPAB, who regarded the very fabric of such buildings as inviolable. One founder member of the Society and a former pupil of Scott himself, John James Stevenson, explained the Society's position in a paper entitled *Architectural Restoration: Its Principles and Practice*, which he read before the Royal Institute of British Architects. Here he took 'instances from the practice of Sir Gilbert Scott, Mr Street and others, whose standing and eminence are a guarantee that their work is a favourable example of the system' to illustrate his point. This was the argument:

> The historical monuments of the country are the property not of any one man or of any one age, but of the race; and no single person or generation which has them in its keeping for the time, has the right to destroy them or falsify them.

To give Scott his due, many of the post-Reformation fittings at Bath Abbey had been removed earlier by G P Manners in his restoration of 1833. Yet Scott did remove the galleries and reposition the stone choir screen and it was just such excoriation, the removal of 'wall linings, pavements, flooring, galleries, high pews, partitions, and the introduction of other encumberances as may conceal the ancient work, provided they be clearly modern', to which Stevenson and his fellow SPAB members were opposed.

A much greater problem than stripping out was that of conjectural restoration, and of this there is much evidence at Bath. The first *Report* of the Bath Abbey Church Restoration Committee, in 1865, records that 'new battlements have been erected of the design which is considered to have been originally intended'. The evidence was contained in publications such as John Carter's *Some Account of the Abbey Church of Bath* published by the Society of Antiquaries of London in 1798 [152] which show the building as it

152 Bath Abbey, west elevation

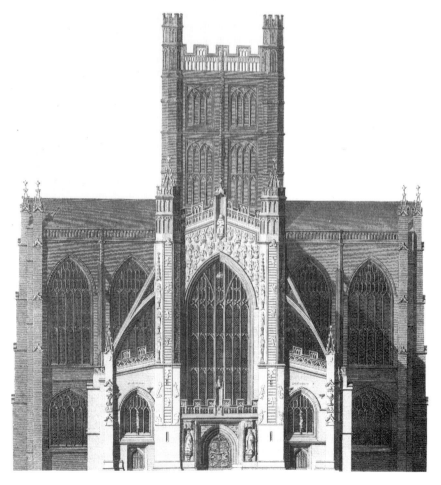

153 Bath Abbey, ceiling plan

[152–153] John Carter's *Account of the Abbey Church of Bath*, published in 1798, shows the Abbey before the nineteenth-century church restorers got to it. In 1833 George Phillips Manners was to add flying buttresses to the nave and rebuild the battlements and the pinnacles and in 1860 Sir Gilbert Scott was to replace the pannelled nave ceiling with stone vaulting.

was before Manners' restoration. In the event Scott stripped off not only Manners' battlements, which were somewhat less elaborate and similar to those at St John the Baptist, Batheaston [114], but also Manners' pinnacles from the west end, and replaced them with shorter, open work pinnacles, closer in design to the original. It should be noted, however, that he left Manners' pinnacles on the tower and the east end [150].

It was inside the Abbey that Scott gave his imagination greatest rein. In his letter to the Rector of 1860 Scott had commented that 'the ceiling, though no doubt intended to be of stone, is really of plaster'. Perhaps in response to this, the 1865 *Report* even suggests that the ceiling of the nave is of an inferior design. Yet whatever the arguments, it is hard to accept that the elaborate plaster ceiling was anything but intended. John Carter's drawings of 1798 [153] show the nave ceiling to be panelled, each bay being divided into four rows of lozenge shaped panels running ten deep from east to west. Although the drawings show this ceiling to be lower than that of the choir, there was little cause for its expensive replacement with stone vaulting. Its condition might have been unsound, but should that have been reason for its total removal? Even if the evidence suggested that it had been the original intention to fan vault the nave and the aisles, contingencies at that time had necessitated its building in timber and plaster. Furthermore, Carter's ceiling plan shows the transepts to be already fan vaulted – but, presumably, this was done in plaster, so Scott did it over in stone.

When Scott responded to Stevenson's attack, it was not without a little pathos:

> Why I – who have laid myself out to protest against the havoc which has been made through the length and breadth of the land under the name of Restoration – should be singled out as the special butt of this yet stronger protest, is not easy to say.

In an attempt to lessen the seriousness of his crime, he cites the elder John Wood as a *bête noir* of church restoration for his work at Llandaff Cathedral in 1734–52. He admits his own mistakes and appears willing to take his share of the blame. But he does maintain that 'the great majority of ancient buildings are committed to the mercy of a herd who trample them under their feet and turn again and rend all objectors'. But such attitudes were going to change.

Some twenty-five years later, in March 1901, the Executive Committee of the Bath Abbey Fabric Fund met in the Guildhall to appoint an architect for further repairs to the Abbey. 'We did not want an architect', announced Sir Richard Paget, 'that would make the Abbey "smick, smack, smooth", but one who would say "lightly touch, 'tis hallowed stone". Such a one we have found in Mr Jackson.' Indeed, Mr Jackson had already proved his worth.

Thomas Graham Jackson, another pupil of Sir Gilbert Scott, had been approached two years earlier, in 1899, to prepare a confidential *Report on Exterior Masonry and Sculpture*. This had been published on 13 July that year and had recommended rather extensive cosmetic work to the west front. The parapets, west gable and central canopy were in need of repair. Four new figures were required at the top of the sculptural ladder and many of the other statues needed copper ties or pins. The figure in the central niche above the west window was missing its head and the figure above the west door was missing altogether. There was also considerable decay in the stonework and the repair of the label or dripmoulds to the west window and the treating of the sculpture in the spandrels with a preservative solution were recommended.

Rapid decay seemed to be a problem which devilled the stonework at Bath Abbey. 'The whole church,' Jackson commented, 'has now pierced open battlemented parapets and pinnacles, the work, I suppose of Sir G G Scott, in 1869. They are still in very fine repair, though many of the pinnacles are beginning to decay.' So Jackson recommended a change of stone:

> I have no confidence in the durability of Bath stone, and should advise the use of a harder material. Clipsham stone, from Rutland, is a splendid oolite, extremely hard and durable, and not so dissimilar in appearance to your local oolite as to be unsuitable, and I should recommend you to use it in preference to any of your local stones. The behaviour of the Bath stone put in at the repairs of 1869 confirms me in making this recommendation.

The estimated cost of these works was £1,310. For this sum Jackson 'provided for employing a really good sculptor for the figure work, and not leaving it, as is so often done, to architectural carvers.' [154] The sculptor was to be his fellow Royal Academician, Sir George Frampton. The work, which Jackson undertook, was finished in early 1901 and the dedication service held in June that year.

Jackson's initial instructions had related only to the preservation of the fabric. Such an approach had elicited a very favourable response from the new secretary of SPAB, Thackeray Turner. In March 1899 he had written:

> The Society for the Protection of Ancient Buildings is glad to find from the appeal issued by Canon Quirk, the Rector of Bath, that 'repair rather than restoration' is to be the character of the proposed work at the Abbey Church.

But a further report by the Executive Committee, published in November 1900 in response to recommendations made by Jackson, made three requests which were hardly just repair and might have met with the disapproval of SPAB. Firstly, that the flying buttresses on the south east aisle were repaired and rebuilt where necessary: secondly, that a new figure was placed in the uppermost niche on the west front 'instead of replacing a new head to this dilapidated statue as originally proposed': and thirdly, to build two new flying buttresses at the west end of the nave to correspond with those at the east end of the choir. Jackson undertook the work which was completed by 1904.

These more substantial repairs proved to be the beginning of a series of works which were to keep Jackson employed at Bath Abbey for twenty-five years. In 1906 he added eight new pinnacles, replacing those of both Manners and Scott [155]. In 1912 he built the organ and organ loft in the north transept [156] and finally, in 1923, added the War Memorial cloister against the south aisle [157]. This cloister was completed by 1924 at a cost of £5,021 and was opened and dedicated on Armistice Day, 1927.

In all these works, but most particularly in the cloister, Jackson employed a Gothic which conformed to the nature of the Abbey. But, as he had argued in *Modern Gothic Architecture* (1873), this was not 'Gothic in its dotage', but Perpendicular 'treated, it need

155 Bath Abbey, new pinnacles

154 Bath Abbey, restoration work to west front

156 Bath Abbey, organ and organ loft

157 Bath Abbey, proposed new cloister

[154–157] In 1900 Sir Thomas Graham Jackson started his restoration of Bath Abbey with repair work to the west front. In 1906 he added eight new pinnacles, replacing the six by George Phillips Manners on the tower and east end and the two by Sir Gilbert Scott on the west end. In 1912 he built the new organ and organ loft in the north transept and in 1923 added the War Memorial Cloister against the south aisle. This cloister was very similar to one he had proposed for Winchester Cathedral in 1910 but which had never been built.

scarcely be said, in a very different spirit and more scientific way than in the time of Pugin'. Jackson was not building Gothic for the sake of Gothic. Indeed, he found little to recommend in the Gothic Revival:

> It must be confessed that the Gothic movement, in spite of all the good it has done, has failed as yet to produce anything approaching to the general recovery of art to a healthy state which is its proper end.

Jackson used Gothic in an attempt to provide a recognisably modern architecture. As he put it, 'We claim the right, as we become more used to the style, to mould and fashion it to suit the modern world, as fast and as freely as the growth of our artistic powers will enable us.'

While employed at Bath Jackson wrote *Reason in Architecture* (1906) and here he separates stylistic appearance from spiritual intent:

> It has been the fault of all revivals of bygone styles that what has been imitated was not the motive principle but the outward details of the style. . . It was with the externals of the style that they dealt, and by mere precedent that they were governed.

It can be argued that this is how his work at Bath differs from both Manners' and Scott's: whereas they, essentially, were restoring, Jackson was building anew. As he said in *Reason in Architecture*:

> It is the Art of Today that should be of the first consequence, and our study of the Arts of our forefathers should not be a matter of mere historical research however interesting, but such as will enable us to catch the spirit that inspired it, and in that spirit to do better work of our own.

In this, the SPAB surely would have approved.

CHAPTER 6

Variegated Architecture for the Mid-century

THE ITALIAN PALAZZO STYLE

The Italian Palazzo style had been introduced to Britain by Charles Barry in 1829, at the Travellers Club in Pall Mall, London. Between 1817 and 1820 Barry had undertaken an extensive continental tour and his detailed studies of the Renaissance architecture of Rome and Florence proved to be the basis of his later success. His early work, following his return, had been in the Greek (the Royal Institution of Fine Arts, Manchester, 1824) and the Gothic (St Peter, Brighton, 1824) styles prevalent at the time. But at the Travellers Club he introduced something which was free of the chaste simplicity of the Greek and the unarchaeological wildness of the Gothic. The Italian Palazzo style was based on the domestic architecture of Renaissance Italy and offered the architect the opportunity of exploiting a greater richness of detail which was to appeal so strongly to his generation.

Once introduced the success of the style was confirmed in the building Barry designed in 1837 for the adjacent site, the Reform Club. At the Travellers Club, the style had appealed to the cosmopolitan awareness of the membership, and now at the Liberals' Reform Club, it was seen to represent something new and different to the images of state and church found in contemporary architecture.

In the same way as the Travellers Club was based on Raphael's Palazzo Pandolfini in Florence (1520), the Reform Club was based, without doubt, on the Palazzo Farnese in Rome [158]. Begun by Sangallo in 1530 and with the top floor added by Michaelangelo in 1546, the Farnese was the grandest Roman palace of its time. It would seem that Barry was out to flatter, if not stun, his clients

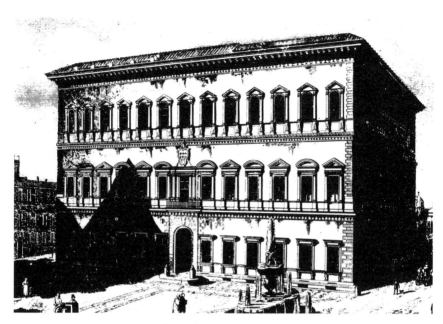

158 The Palazzo Farnese, Rome

with his design. The Palazzo style was significant in that it differed from the Palladian, the basis of so much street architecture in London and Bath, in the arrangement of the elevation [159]. Equal weight or importance was given to each of the principle storeys – no longer were the *piano rustica* and the *piano nobile* so individually expressed – and the whole elevation was bound in by heavily rusticated quoins at the corners and a deep, crowning cornice supporting the roof. Barry took the expression of this enclosing framework further by extending the corners of the building through the roof in the form of chimneys. The manner in which the windows were treated also differed greatly from the Palladian. No longer was the façade divided by columns or pilasters with arched or pedimented windows set between: unadorned, the façade was now astylar and each window was presented as an aedicule, an opening with side columns or pilasters supporting a pedimented entablature. The effect was much more of a plain banded façade interrupted by window openings and highlighted by areas of rich and varied decoration. In strict architectural terms, it was an historical regression from the Palladian, but it provided a suitable expression, in its richness of detail, of the confidence and wealth of the newly emergent middle classes.

While work was still being completed on the Reform Club a

159 The Reform Club, Pall Mall, London

London architect, George Alexander, brought the Italian Palazzo style to Bath. In 1840–41 Alexander built the Savings Bank, now the Registry Office, in Charlotte Street [160]. It is important as a very early example of the Italian Palazzo style outside London, and it is probably also the first adaptation of its use to a bank: the style was

160 The Bath Savings Bank, Charlotte Street
[158–160] The Palazzo Farnese, started by Sangallo in 1530 and finished off by Michelangelo in 1546 was the model for Sir Charles Barry's Reform Club of 1837. This, in turn, was the source of George Alexander's Bath Savings Bank of 1840–41.

then used for clubhouses. Although only three bays wide and three storeys high, the weight of this building is intense and the late-Georgian terraces along Charlotte Street appear thin by comparison. In his elevations Alexander returns more strictly to the Italian precedents by alternating triangular and semi-circular pediments above the windows, as done at both the Palazzi Farnese and Pandolfini. This move was not proposed by Barry until he designed the British Embassy in Constantinople in 1842. In execution, Alexander's design lacked the richness of decoration he had intended and the Palladian porch which now mars the street front, lacks any of the plastic qualities of either the original design or the Italian inspiration.

In London the Italian Palazzo style devolved into the ornate, speculative Italianate of the Kensington terraces, but Bath did not need terraces as London did. By the end of the first quarter of the nineteenth century the terraced expansion of the city was complete. Furthermore, the demand was increasingly for detached and private residences. This was first evidenced, as Tony Walter writing on *The Decline of the Georgian Terrace* has pointed out, through the strange about face done by Widcombe Terrace and Widcombe Crescent (both c.1805), where the buildings do not address so much the city but their own private landscapes. What was now called for were villas on the surrounding hills and for this the Palazzo style was unsuitable. By the same argument the Italian Villa style found little favour in west London where the demand was largely for terraces.

It was inevitable that, as architects used the Palazzo and Villa styles more often and with increasingly less discretion, they would merge into a common Italianate which ultimately became so representative of much nineteenth-century architecture. An example of this is the corner building on the Sawclose and Westgate Street, until recently The County Wine Vaults [161]: here the style is a confusion of Palazzo and Villa images, but at least the building deals with the corner successfully.

In this context Charles Edward Davis must be introduced, the City Architect, who dominated the local architectural scene for much of the latter half of the century. As architect and archaeologist he did much to change the face of Bath and his work, often quite diverse in style, can be seen from almost every corner.

Typical of Davis' exuberant Italianate was the block on the north side of Quiet Street which he refaced in 1871. More controlled and a few years earlier is the small Police Station and Lock-up [162] he

161 The County Wine Vaults, Sawclose and Westgate Street

162 The Police Station, Orange Grove

[161–162] Italian Palazzo and Villa architecture fused together in a common Italianate at the corner of Sawclose and Westgate Streets and in Charles Edward Davis' Police Station of 1865. The arched screen adjacent to the Police Station came with John McKean Brydon's Guildhall Extension of 1893 [217].

built on the north of the Orange Grove in 1865. The heavy rustication of the *piano rustica* gives the building a suitably strong and formidable appearance which, with the round headed windows above and the overhanging eaves, recalls the rear façade of Barry's Travellers Club of many years before. In its day, this building would have stood out, a squat symbol of law and order, between a motley collection of Georgian buildings which flanked the site. But now, squeezed in between the Guildhall extension and the vast Empire Hotel, it appears diminutive and lost.

THE FRENCH RENAISSANCE STYLE

The French Renaissance, or Modern French as it was called, was, in a way, a natural development from the Italianate Classicism of the mid-nineteenth century and in that sense it followed the course of history. These years saw the creation of the Second Empire in France, the Paris Exhibition of 1844, and the building of Visconti and Lefuel's opulent addition to the Louvre in Paris, between 1852 and 1870 [163].

Meanwhile in England French Renaissance *chateaux* were coming from the offices of the country house architects, but it was a style most usually chosen by the *nouveau-riche*. The first appearance of the French Renaissance style in urban architecture was at Montague House in Whitehall, built between 1853 and 1859 for the Scottish Duke of Buccleuch by his Scottish architect, William Burn. It was a style that was grand and palatial, both in effect and by association, and it was instantly adopted by the new hotels, often the product of the railways, which by the mid-1860s were appearing across the London skyline. The first was J T Knowles' Grosvenor Hotel at Victoria Station [164], built in 1860. This was followed by the London Bridge Hotel (1861), the Westminster Palace Hotel (1863), the Charing Cross Hotel (1863) and the Langham Hotel (1864), and others. If they were not actually French Renaissance in style they were tall and featured broken skylines. For it was the richness of decoration and the varied form of the skylines – high Mansard roofs, chimneys and dormers – which held the appeal. It was seen as a relief from the heavy brooding cornices of the Italianate buildings which tended to impart a regularity to a city skyline devoid of interest, vigour and

163 The Louvre, Paris

164 The Grosvenor Hotel, Victoria Station, London

[163–164] Visconti and Lefuel's opulent addition to the Louvre in 1852–70 generated great interest in French Renaissance architecture. This was reflected by J T Knowles in the Grosvenor Hotel which he built in 1860 at Victoria Station – just where the boat-train from France came in.

even the Picturesque. It also played a role in the developing debate known as 'The Battle of the Styles'. Although essentially a Classical style, it represented, in its lively silhouette, a victory of sorts for the Gothicists, for they felt that Classical architecture was now being forced to stress the features which they, the Gothicists, recognised as important.

It was logical that French Renaissance should find favour in hotel buildings. In Paris the French lived in large apartment blocks: in London the English did not. Therefore, the correlation between multiple occupancy dwellings – the situation which the new hotels represented – and the French Renaissance style of the new Parisian apartments was clear. Thus it is not surprising that the one big hotel built in Bath in the mid-nineteenth century, gave a lively taste of the French Renaissance, the Grand Pump Room Hotel.

Won in competition in 1867 by William Willcox, the partner of James Wilson, the Grand Pump Room Hotel was the most supreme expression of mid-Victorian self confidence that Bath ever saw. Located on Stall Street, directly across from the Pump Room and Abbey, it disregarded the Pump Room rather less than Pump Room had, in its turn, disregarded the Abbey. Sadly it was demolished in 1959 and the buildings which now stand on its site

165 The Grand Pump Room Hotel, Stall Street, winning competition entry

NEW BATHS AND PUMP-ROOM HOTEL, BATH.

166 The Grand Pump Room Hotel, Stall Street
[165–166] William Willcox's winning entry for the 1867 Grand Pump Room Hotel competition was not built. What Wilson and Willcox did build was a muted and far less joyful version of the first – but rather that than the appallingly faceless architecture which has now replaced it.

between Westgate Street and Bath Street are a poor excuse for such urban vandalism.

Formed around three sides of a courtyard the original design [165] for the building was varied and expressive in arrangement. Across the open side of the quadrangle ran a screen with a large pedimented entrance, boldly reflecting the Pump Room colonnade opposite, built across the end of the Abbey churchyard by Thomas Baldwin in 1786. Baldwin's pediment is decorated, in its tympanum, with sphinxes on either side of an oval wreath, and this would seem to have been the theme adopted by Willcox. The hotel in fact made further concessions to the Pump Room opposite: the arrangement of a vermiculated, rusticated ground floor surmounted by twinned, engaged Corinthian columns was employed and it was only above the entablature at third floor level that the design really began to fill out. It was a rather muted version [166] of this winning design which was eventually built

167 25 Marlborough Buildings

but, considering its location, the Pump Room Hotel was almost guaranteed success. And Wilson, Willcox and Wilson, as they became, returned to extend the building in 1872 and to make further alterations in 1890–91.

Elsewhere in Bath, the French Renaissance made little impact, but a couple of domestic schemes are worth commenting upon. Noticeable, simply because it does not fit in, is the four storey porch on the front of no. 25 Marlborough Buildings [167]. Whereas its neighbours might rise to three storeys, stopping just short of the cornice, this one breaks through that line with a tall, Mansard roof and, overlooking the street, a rich oculus or bulls-eye window. Of further interest here are the cast-iron shafts placed in

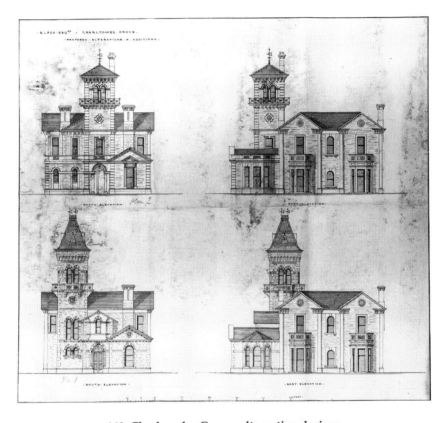

168 Charlcombe Grove, alternative designs
[167–168] Palladian terraces and, latterly, Italianate villas were so endemic in Bath that domestic excursions into other styles, whether French Renaissance or Italian Gothic, never seem particularly comfortable.

front of the first floor window: in such a French context one is reminded of the remarkable cast-iron designs in Eugene Viollet-le-Duc's *Entretiens Sur l'Architecture* (1863).

In c1860 James Wilson offered a rather French Renaissance-cum-Italian Gothic design as an alternative to the Italian Villa style for alterations and additions at Charlcombe Grove [168]. The existing house, it would seem, was a small building, with two cross-gables, in the Italian Villa style. The intention was to build a tower and to add rooms to the south elevation, thus providing a new entrance and probably a hall or billiard room. The first option was to do this in the existing Italianate manner, using details much as Loudon might have suggested. The alternative was to employ a strange combination of French Mansard roof, and machicolations and polychromatic windows in the Italian Gothic manner. If nothing else, this combination would have conformed to Hussey's conception of the Picturesque.

THE TUDOR AND JACOBETHAN STYLES

Whereas the Picturesque had developed, initially, from images drawn from the Italian *campagna*, the architecture which eventually found its way into the movement embraced, as Hussey has suggested, a whole range of styles. The *cottages ornées* which

169 *A Gothic Cottage*

170 Hardwicke Hall, Derbyshire

[169–170] While pattern books, such as John Buonarotti Papworth's *Rural Residences*, popularised the domestic architecture of Tudor and Jacobethan England, folios, such as Joseph Nash's *Mansions of England in the Olden Times*, romantised the lifestyle of those times.

were illustrated in the pattern books, such as J B Papworth's *Rural Residences* (1818, 1832) [169], were as often as not based upon late-mediaeval English domestic architecture: indeed, such sources provide the stylistic basis for John Nash's cottages at Blaise Hamlet at Henbury (1810–11) and Edward Davis' Gothic Farm House in the Royal Victoria Park at Bath.

The choice of such late-Gothic and early-Renaissance styles, Tudor, Elizabethan and Jacobean – or Tudor and Jacobethan – was based more upon patriotic sentiment than antiquarian zeal. At a time when the nation had been threatened for many years the need to associate with a time of English strength – the age of Raleigh and Drake, Bacon and Shakespeare – must have been strong. Sir Walter Scott exploited this sentiment in many of his Waverley novels; consider *Kenilworth*, published in 1821.

The Tudor and Jacobethan styles came into their own in the 1830s, the decade of parliamentary and religious reform. This decade saw a considerable number of architectural publications, starting with Thomas Frederick Hunt's *Exemplars of Tudor Architecture Adapted to Modern Habitations* (1830). This was followed in 1833 by Thomas Hutchings Clarke's *Domestic*

Architecture of the Reigns of Queen Elizabeth and James I. In the same
year J C Loudon published his *Encyclopedia of Cottage, Farm and
Villa Architecture* and pictured a Jacobethan design as his 'Beau
Ideal of an English Villa'. This was the inspiration of an 'amateur
architect, residing in Wiltshire', which had been revised for
publication by Charles Barry. Charles James Richardson, a pupil of
Sir John Soane, produced studies of Tudor and Jacobethan
architecture in 1837, 1840 and 1841 but probably the most famous
of the books of this time, and the most lasting, was Joseph Nash's
The Mansions of England in the Olden Times. Published in four
volumes between 1839 and 1849 these books illustrated, in rich
reproductions, an old England of warmth and hospitality, in a
Tudor setting [170]. His marvellously atmospheric drawings of the
busy life of Elizabethan mansions served to popularise the period
far more than the academic studies which had preceded it. Nash
provided an image which supported and recalled Sir Walter
Scott's prose of some twenty years before. And in doing so Nash
stirred an innate nationalism which often went beyond sen-
timentality to entrenched Toryism.

Thus this resurgence of interest in old England can be seen as a
countermovement in this decade of reform. The Tudor and
Jacobethan styles largely came from the great country houses,
Longleat, for instance, or Hardwick Hall, and it was in new
country house architecture that it first made its reappearance.
Anthony Salvin began Harlaxton Hall in Lincolnshire in 1831, a
great Jacobethan house, in the style which Loudon described two
years later as his 'Beau Ideal'. It was the adoption of the Tudor and
Jacobethan by the Tory establishment which promoted it as the
only viable alternative to the new style of clubhouses and banks,
the Italian Palazzo. This was the language of the Liberals – the very
name of the Reform Club was evidence enough – and the landed
and suburban Tories sought refuge in something familiar and
nationalistic in their architecture.

When the old Houses of Parliament were destroyed by fire in
1834 it was announced that the new building, to be won in
competition, had to be in the Gothic or Elizabethan styles. This
was as much to suggest an expression of nationalistic sentiment,
as a blending with Westminster Hall or nearby Westminster
Abbey. All but six of the ninety-seven entries were in the
prescribed styles and the winners were Sir Charles Barry and A W
N Pugin. Yet the Tudor and Jacobethan styles were not cared for by
many of the leading architects. Even C J Richardson, in

Observations on the Architecture of England During the Reigns of Queen Elizabeth and James I (1837), commented: 'I do not desire that it should become extensively adopted'. It was thought to be neither one thing nor the other, neither Classical nor Gothic. In much the same way as the Palladians of the eighteenth century had rejected it for being ignorant, the Gothicists of the nineteenth century were to rebuke it for being degenerate. The first recorder of the *History of the Gothic Revival*, Charles Eastlake, wrote in 1872: 'It requires no great discernment on the part of modern critics to perceive both in the Tudor and Elizabethan styles abundant evidence of a fallen art.' Yet the Tudor and Jacobethan survived, although admittedly in the shade, largely because they were English and convenient.

The convenience of the styles lay in both their arrangement and their decoration. Symmetry of plan could be dispensed with to the supposedly greater convenience of the arrangement, and large mullioned and transomed windows, so much a feature of the styles, let in an abundance of light and air. And there was the advantage of cheapness: Jacobethan, or indeed Tudor, could work as well at Harlaxton, in all its decorated grandeur, as they could in the many hospitals and workhouses, devoid of decoration, which grew up following the Poor Law Reform Act of 1834.

It is in this context that Tudor architecture was first reintroduced at Bath. Surprisingly, it was not used for the workhouse – that was built in a late Classical style to the design of Sampson Kempthorne at a cost of £6,440 and opened for the accommodation of 1029 poor people in 1838: it is now the core of St Martin's Hospital. It was G P Manners who, as City Architect, introduced a rather collegiate version of the style in the new building for the recently displaced St Catherine's Hospital, Beau Street [171], which he rebuilt in 1829. The minimal decoration which consisted of no more than dripmoulds to the windows and door, and the simplest of cornices, indicates how cheaply the style could be carried out. The building has a certain dignity in its symmetry which is indicative of the architect's Classical training. Manners followed this, two years later, with designs for rebuilding Bellot's Hospital [172] on the opposite side of Beau Street.

Although the accommodation remained very basic and the style Tudor, Manners allowed himself more decoration than he had done previously at St Catherine's Hospital. The central entrance bay on the west front is strongly expressed between polygonal

171 St Catherine's Hospital, Beau Street

172 Bellot's Hospital, Beau Street, unbuilt elevations

[171–172] A rather collegiate Tudor architecture was used by George Phillips Manners at St Catherine's Hospital in 1829 and again, but with more ornamentation, in his designs for Bellot's Hospital of 1831.

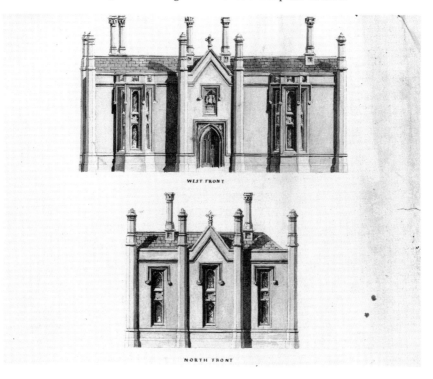

WEST FRONT

NORTH FRONT

buttresses and the feeling of symmetry is reinforced by the strongly articulated bay windows. This design, however, was not implemented and Bellot's Hospital was not rebuilt until 1859, and then by Cotterell and Spackman.

The suitability of Tudor and Jacobethan for school or collegiate buildings was not in doubt. Henry Hakewell had suggested the style at Rugby School, Warwickshire (1809–15) and C R Cockerell, a renowned Classicist, had employed it successfully at Harrow, Middlesex (1819–20) and, on a far grander scale, at St David's College, Lampeter (1822–27). Yet they were doing little more than following mediaeval collegiate precedents, whether they be St John's College, Oxford (1511) or the Charterhouse, London (1545).

Before the mid-century the Tudor style had been adopted for schools in Bath. Manners, then on his own, had used it at Beacon Hill School in c1839 and next at St Michael's School in c1841. Then about ten years later James Wilson did the same for the Trinity Parochial School. So there must have been little surprise when Wilson built Kingswood College on Lansdown [173] in 1851, for the sons of Wesleyan ministers, in a hefty, symmetrical early-Tudor style. He even allowed himself, in the treatment of the

173 Kingswood College, Lansdown   James Wilson's Tudor design of 1851 for Kingswood College draws upon well-established sixteenth- and nineteenth-century precedents for collegiate buildings

174 St Swithin's Almshouses, Lansdown

top of the tower, some touches of Somerset Perpendicular. Both the style and arrangement are not dissimilar to what he had done ten years earlier at Cheltenham College.

It was a similar, collegiate, early-Tudor style which Wilson had chosen for St Swithen's Almshouses [174], to be built on the slopes of Lansdown, just below St Stephen's Church, in 1842. The

175 St Swithin's Almshouses, Lansdown, elevation
[174–175] Only six out of the sixteen almshouses designed by James Wilson in 1843 were built. Today there is little about these buildings, now known as St Stephen's Villas, to suggest the extensiveness of this grandly collegiate conception.

concept was rather grand [175]: a central chapel and hall, flanked by two ranges of eight almshouses. Each house was clearly defined by its triangular gable and cluster of chimneys, but once again the design is subjected to the strong symmetry of the Classically trained architect. In the event only six almshouses were built and, as St Stephen's Villas, produce a charming composition.

It was G P Manners again, now in association with J Elkington Gill who, in 1859–60, built the Bluecoat School [176] in the Sawclose. But now the architecture is later and, in its clear incorporation of Classical features, noticeably Jacobethan. There are decorated gables, engaged columns and very rich, ornamental strapwork. This latter treatment, popular in early Renaissance work [177], embodies not only the school crest, but in the central bay of the north front, the initials of the founder of 1711, Robert Nelson. The incorporation of such lettering in the strapwork is well demonstrated, historically, at Robert Smithson's Hardwick Hall in Derbyshire (1590–97). As a nineteenth-century building the Bluecoat School is more than a little contrived and self conscious. The combination of Classical and non-Classical elements strives for the Picturesque rather than historical authenticity and the building's rather forced asymmetry is not wholly convincing.

Tudor and Jacobethan were styles with which architects such as Manners and Wilson felt at home even if the spokesmen of the profession would rather eschew them. This can be most clearly seen in the number of villas built in the many new suburban developments around the city. The style, simplified to meet the meanest purse, could work as well for the detached villa, such as Wonham on Lansdown (1848) [178] as it could for the semi-detached pair (designed c1841) [179]. A more expensive version

176 The Bluecoat School, Sawclose

177 Blickling Hall, Norfolk
[176–177] Drawing upon
sources such as Blickling Hall,
Norfolk (here dating from
1620), illustrated in Henry
Shaw's *Details of Elizabethan
Architecture*, George Phillips
Manners and J Elkington Gill
built the ornately Jacobethan
Bluecoat School in 1859–60.

178 Wonham, Lansdown Road
179 Design for semi-detached houses

EAST ELEVATION

180 Abbey Rectory, Park Lane

181 Raglan Villas, Wells Road

[178–181]Where patriotism was preferred to the Picturesque, Tudor and Jaco-bethan villas were to be seen studding the hillsides around Bath. From the simplicity of James Wilson's semi-detached pair of c1841, or single villas such as Wonham of 1848, the vocabulary could be developed to suit ornate and complex buildings such as Abbey Rectory of 1849 or Raglan Villas built, as the name would suggest, in c1856.

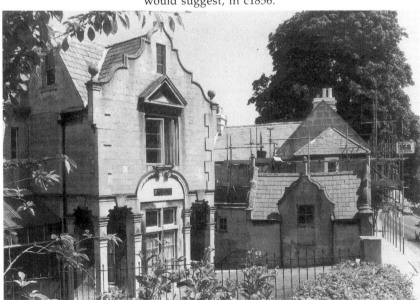

might be Abbey Rectory on Park Lane (1849) [180] or Raglan Villas on the Wells Road (c 1856) [181].

In 1827 Edward Davis, while restoring the Grenville Monument on Lansdown, built five Tudor villas on Entry Hill Drive. One, called Granville (sic), bears insignia from the monument. These houses were exhibited at the Royal Academy in 1828 as 'now building' and it would seem likely that it was Davis, architect of his own house at 6 South Hayes in this style, who added the pair of fine lodges at the east end of the North Parade Bridge in 1835–6 [182]. They are the best example of the Jacobethan readily seen in Bath and the details, particularly the strapwork, are very well preserved. The Bridge was built, at this time, to the designs of W Tierney Clark, an engineer, but the Jacobethan lodges are much more elaborate and thus stand out from this rather Palladian design.

182 North Parade Bridge, lodges   In 1835–36 Edward Davis added these richly Jacobethan lodges to W Tierney Clark's more mundane bridge.

183 Bath Spa Station

THE GREAT WESTERN RAILWAY

The largest single development in the Tudor style was, however, not the making of a Bath architect but an outside company, the Great Western Railway, and their style proliferated from Paddington to Temple Meads, Bristol.

The first locomotives ran into the station now called Bath Spa on 31st August 1840. They came from Bristol, for that was the only part of the line yet open. It was not until the end of June 1841 that trains were running the whole length of the line from Bristol to London. The importance of Bristol as a terminus for the railway should be noted, for it was in Bristol, the leading port of entry for the west of England, that much of the work that led to the establishing of the railway was done.

In 1833 Isambard Kingdom Brunel had become engineer to the Great Western Railway, forming a connection which lasted until his death in 1859. Brunel has been noted for his extraordinary keeness of mind, perseverance, originality and his inclination to do things on a grand scale. The great Box Tunnel to the east of Bath bears witness to this.

184 Temple Meads Station, Bristol
[183–184] The extensive station roofs which Isambard Kingdom Brunel built
for the Great Western Railway at Bath Spa and Bristol Temple Meads in 1840,
were not, as they would appear to be, of hammer-beam construction.

Brunel's hand in the railway station at Bath was to be seen in the
great roof which once spanned the lines and the platforms alike,
the skew bridge over the Avon and possibly the viaduct running
towards Twerton. The roof at Bath [183] was, in appearance, a
great, Gothic hammer-beam structure, and not at all dissimilar to
that which still stands at Bristol, Temple Meads [184], although it
no longer shelters trains. Yet neither of these roofs were quite
what they seemed to be; the Tudor appearance was for mere effect.
Although the roof at Bath was very modest in expression, that at
Bristol seems to spring into mediaeval life with pendentives and
traceried spandrels.

Both these roofs were illustrated by J C Bourne in his *History and
Description of the Great Western Railway* in 1846. The description he
gives fits both Bath and Bristol and makes it clear that neither was
of a hammer-beam construction:

The roof is particularly well suited to the purpose to which it
is applied, and it covers a clear span of 74 feet, without the aid

of either cross tie or abutment. . . It is composed of a series of 44 ribs, 22 on each side, and placed 10 feet apart, each of which is constructed somewhat like the jib of a crane, that is to say, of a long arm, projecting far and rising high into the air, and a short arm or tail. . . In the present case, the iron columns which divide the central space from the aisles are the fulcra or crane posts upon which the arms rest. The long arm or jib extends to the centre and ridge of the roof, and then meets its fellow from the opposite side, while the short arm or tail is carried backward to form the roof of the aisle. . . The whole is then planked over diagonally, and is intended to be filled up and decorated to suit the rest of the building.

The main station building, unlike Bristol, had little Tudor to recommend it. It was, in fact, a fairly plain building on two floors, the heavy stone mullions and first floor oriel window being really the only manifestations of a Tudor style. The building remains virtually unaltered today, at least externally, save for the later sympathetic addition of the rather Jacobethan ornamental gables over the three central bays.

The Skew Bridge immediately to the west of the station was built by Brunel in 1840. It was remarkable for both its form and its materials. The bridge had two spans each of 89 feet and each span was made up of six parallel ribs at five feet centres. These ribs were of laminated Baltic timber from Memel, each lamination 6 inches thick and the whole fastened by iron bolts and straps. The use of laminated timber arches had been decided on due to construction delays and problems in the competitive tenders for the original design for an iron bridge. Masonry piers now supported the twin spans and the spandrels of the outside arches were filled with ornamental cast-iron in a type of early-Tudor panel tracery, this in turn supporting a timber parapet. This bridge was unique, being Brunel's only use of laminated timber in bridge construction. When the bridge was replaced in 1878, it had exceeded its life expectancy by some thirteen years.

The Skew Bridge led straight into the viaduct [185], which was turreted and castellated and gave the appearance of being part of the ancient wall of the city, except that it was facing the wrong way, and its early-Tudor coat is a thin and two dimensional affair. It is, indeed, no more Gothic in its construction than the roof of the station or the spandrels of the skew bridge. One recalls Pugin's maxim in *True Principles* and sees that there is everything about

185 The railway viaduct

186 'Railway bridges on the antient principles'

[185–186] Writing in his *Apology for the Revival of Christian Architecture in England* in 1843, A W N Pugin criticised the Great Western Railway for their 'mock castellated work, huge tracery, shields without bearings, no meaning projections, and all sorts of unaccountable breaks'. He would have had railway bridges designed 'on the antient principles' of the late-thirteenth century.

these structures that is not necessary for convenience, construction or propriety.

In the viaduct the stonework is a mere facing, the inside of the turrets displaying, at platform level, a solid lining of brickwork. The whole of the emphasis is on the north side facing the city – the south side facing Beechen Cliff is almost devoid of battlements, buttresses and bastions. Furthermore, the composition is controlled in a traditionally Classical manner. Like the river front of the Palace of Westminster, it is symmetrical about a central axis: tower reflects tower; archway, archway; buttress, buttress. The symmetry is accentuated by the centrally placed shields which, like the flanking towers, stand proud of the smooth line of battlements. Pugin was not impressed by such a use of Gothic, even such late-Gothic as Tudor. In his 1843 *Apology for the Revival of Christian Architecture in England* Pugin wrote:

> The Great Western stations, where any architectural display has been attempted, are mere caricatures of pointed design, – mock castellated work, huge tracery, shields without bearings, no-meaning projections, and all sorts of unaccountable breaks, to make up a design at once costly, and offensive, and full of pretension.

Then rather confusingly, Pugin cites Rugby (Midland) Station on the LNWR as an example of this practice. 'The old station had four half-turrets with the west side turned out, and a few sham loopholes' because, so he says, Rugby School as recently rebuilt by Hakewell had similar thin Tudor trimmings.

Pugin regarded the railways as a great opportunity for the implementation of a true, simple Gothic architecture [186]. They were of the nineteenth century and so, he hoped, was the Gothic. The massive Doric arch at Euston was, to his mind, an example of 'Brobdingnagian absurdities'. He made his point in *An Apology* with the use, once again, of comparative illustrations. The text is clear and to the point:

> The railways, had they been naturally treated, afforded a fine scope for grand massive architecture. Little more was required than buttresses, weathering, and segmental arches, resistance to *lateral* and *perpendicular pressure*. I do not hesitate to say, that, by merely following out the work that was required to its natural conclusion, building exactly what

was wanted in the simplest and most substantial manner . . .
tens of thousands of pounds could have been saved on every
line, and grand and durable masses of buildings been
produced.

Bath's GWR station had, like so many others, missed its
opportunity.

THE ROMANESQUE AND
NEO-NORMAN

Bearing in mind the tradition of Tudor architecture for collegiate
and institutional buildings, it is a little surprising that it was really
Romanesque or Neo-Norman designs which both G P Manners
and James Wilson produced, separately, for Queen's College in
1839. Queen's College, an auxiliary to the Universities of Oxford
and Cambridge, was to stand on Claverton, a little lower down
than our present university. It was intended to be a national
Protestant college and, as *The Bath and County Gazette* said, to
'prove a strong bulwark to the Church, disseminating the true
faith, in spite of the efforts of Romanism and Infidelity.' Was this
why the building was sited within possible view of Prior Park? 'It
is admitted,' the paper continued, 'that the Roman Catholics in
this island are making rapid strides for domination: and that our
two Universities are not adequate for all the purposes of enabling
youth to compete with the Roman Priesthood.' Nevertheless, the
new College, to which the Queen had given her approval, was to
be broadly based educationally, offering every department of
science and the fine arts as well as a school of design, a museum
and a library.

James Wilson's design [187] was selected, though why is
unclear. A subscription list was opened in the hope of raising the
£30,000 required, and a painted window and an altarpiece were
promised. Although a foundation stone was laid as early as 1837
and the foundation walls built, the enterprise came to nothing.
Perhaps this was because many of the leading Bath figures were
not shown as promoters and the hoped for support was therefore
not forthcoming. Maybe this is just as well for Wilson's scheme
displayed much of the awkwardness which can be so often

187 Queen's College, Claverton Down, unbuilt design　In 1837 work began on James Wilson's design for a University auxiliary on Claverton Down but got little further than the foundation stone. In the event, that was probably just as well.

188 Queen's College, Claverton Down, unbuilt design

associated with his work – consider St Stephen's or the Royal School.

Whereas Wilson's effort was a rather ambiguous hybrid of Romanesque and Neo-Norman forms – consider the loosely Lombardic but towered end pavilions – Manner's design was a much more convincing attempt at Neo-Norman [188]. (Wilson's confusion is all the more surprising if one looks at the

Neo-Norman chapel he built in Walcot Cemetery a couple of years later). Though doubtless choosing the style because of its fashionable appeal, it would seem likely that Manners was swayed in his decision by a publication that had come out, far ahead of its time, in 1814. This was called *Phantasm of an University* and its author was a Cambridge man, a contemporary of William Wilkins, called Charles Kelsall. He could be compared with Thomas Hope but, as David Watkins has commented in *Thomas Hope and the Neo-Classical Ideal*, his outlook was infinitely more *avant-garde*. His *Phantasm* proposed a drastic reform, both academically and architecturally, of the existing university system: that is, Oxford and Cambridge. He proposed a university of six colleges devoted to six separate fields of study and each was to be in a different architectural style. The one of greatest concern here is the College of Natural Philosophy [189], for it was to be in the style later adopted by Manners for his design for Queen's College: the four storey accommodation ranges are almost identical. The College of Natural Philosophy was composed of what Kelsall considered to be 'the best parts of the few genuine Saxon specimens remaining in England.' It was, in fact, his intention to 'prove that this style of architecture, though destitute of the symmetry which charac-

189 The College of Natural Philosophy, unbuilt design
[188–189] George Phillips Manner's design for a University auxiliary was in the newly fashionable *Rundbogenstil* and was probably influenced by Charles Kelsall's design for a College of Natural Philosophy published in *Phantasm of an University* in 1814.

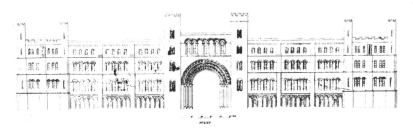

terises the Grecian and pure Roman buildings, becomes nevertheless agreeable if rightly understood and applied.'

In Britain, the Romanesque was made popular for church building by George Ernest Hamilton's *Designs for Rural Churches* (1837) and as such is best seen at James Wilson Wilds' Christ Church at Streatham, London (1840–42) and at Thomas Henry Wyatt and David Grandon's St Mary's Church at Wilton in

190 Lansdown Cemetery   Incorporating piers and railings from around William Beckford's tomb at the Abbey Cemetery [92], H E Goodridge enclosed the newly created cemetery at Lansdown in 1848.

191 Lansdown Cemetery, 'Resurgent'

192 Lansdown Cemetery, 'The Gates of Death'

Wiltshire (1840–46). In Bath there remain two examples, both the work of a now older H E Goodridge. These are the wall and gateway of 1848 to the Lansdown Cemetery and the Independent or Percy Chapel he built with his son, A S Goodridge, in Charlotte Street in 1854.

William Beckford had wanted to be buried in the garden below the Lansdown Tower. But since this was not consecrated ground, it could not be allowed and, as has been noted, he was buried instead in the Abbey Cemetery, behind a wall and railings designed by Goodridge – away from Loudon's structured graveyard. His wish was made possible when his daughter, now the Duchess of Hamilton, repurchased the Tower from its new owner of four months, a publican. Straight away she presented the Tower and the land to the Parish of Walcot and in April 1848, they were consecrated. So now Beckford's remains – and the massive granite sarcophagus he had designed – could be brought from the Abbey Cemetery to the resting ground he had chosen.

It was presumably the Hamiltons who commissioned Goodridge to build the cemetery screen wall [190]: he had already designed a mausoleum for Hamilton Palace in 1841 and again in 1846, and he had so built the enclosure for Beckford's tomb at the Abbey Cemetery [92]. Indeed, it was these same railings and stone piers which formed the flanking elements of the great gateway he built for the new cemetery. The contrast between this screen wall and the Tower is most marked, yet there is something familiar, almost Soanesque, in the sarcophagal forms on the corners of the gabled gateway and atop the piers which flank it. The imagery of death is everywhere. Above the side doors are the mottoes 'Resurgent' [191] and 'The Gates of Death' [192] while in roundels along the wall are winged hour-glasses [193], triangles, crosses and serpents which swallow their tails [194]. These references are, respectively, to 'Father' Time and the Angel of Death, the Trinity, Christianity and Eternity. Many of these symbols were common in contemporary cemetery iconography: the winged hour-glass encircled by the serpent can be seen in the gates to Brompton Cemetery, London (c1840). The architecture is rich, and this is nowhere more noticeable than in the decoration of the main arched entrances [195]. Here there is all the intensity of Byzantine work and, in the individual elements of the decoration, such as the capitals and the spiralling vine motif, distinct attempts at Italian Romanesque. Goodridge probably knew Henry Gally Knights's recent works on Italian Romanesque, *Saracenic and Norman*

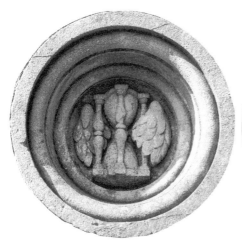

193 Lansdown Cemetery, Time and the Angel of Death

194 Lansdown Cemetery, the Trinity and Eternity

195 Lansdown Cemetery, ornamental gateway
[191–195] Symbolic iconography was mixed with rich Romanesque detailing in the wall and gateway which H E Goodridge built at the Lansdown Cemetery in 1848.

Remains to Illustrate the Normans in Sicily (1838) and *The Ecclesiastical Architecture of Italy from the Time of Constantine to the 15th Century* (1842, 44): he might even have seen Thomas Hopper's extraordinary staircase at Penrhyn Castle, Caernarvonshire (c1825–c1844) to which his own gateway could have been an introduction.

There is less intensity about the Percy Chapel in Charlotte Street [196], built in 1854 in memory of the old client at the Argyle Chapel, Rev William Jay. This church was the result of a dispute over Jay's successor at the Argyle Chapel: Jay, being unhappy at the choice, took a number of his congregation with him on leaving in 1852. Although he died the following year, his congregation had a chapel built near to where he had lived. The style could not have been more different to that of their old church – and this must have been intended – but the galleried building was commodious and ingeniously fitted into the awkward site. The style was unmistakably Lombardic Romanesque and composite of any

196 The Percy Chapel, Charlotte Street, elevation   H E Goodridge, now in collaboration with his son Arthur Goodridge, used Lombardic Romanesque in the Percy Chapel of 1854.

number of eleventh- and twelfth-century examples: again one could consider S Francesca, Brescia. But this church should not be thought of as part of the High-Victorian Italian Gothic interest. Even though it was built the year after the second and third volumes of Ruskin's *Stones of Venice* appeared, it belongs to a movement based on antiquarianism and the Picturesque. There is nothing in the rich, repetitive decoration or the lightweight scale of the church to speak of Ruskin, or the High-Victorian movement in architecture: the choice of symmetrically placed corner towers rather than a *campanile* is evidence enough of this.

SECULAR GOTHIC

There are few secular buildings of any great significance in Bath which can match the accomplishments of Blomfield's St John the Baptist or even Scott's rather less than High-Victorian Gothic St Andrew's. The secular field was just not one which required top class architects in the way churches did: there was not the same prestige, or indeed value, from the client's point of view in having, say, the school house built by a leading London man and anyway, it must have been thought that the local architects could do it just

197 The Convent of La Sainte Union, Pultney Road   J Elkington Gill employed a strongly expressed and carefully asymmetrical design in his convent building for La Sainte Union.

198 The Royal School, Lansdown Originally the Bath and Lansdown Proprietary College, the Royal School, built by James Wilson in 1856–58, displays a confused jumble of fourteenth-century architectural features whose disposition is not helped by the ill-considered massing.

as well. The only exception to this which might be cited is Charles Hansom's presbytery at St John the Divine but this, in its Puginian way, is hardly High Victorian – and it came with the church.

Of the local architects, one name which stands out is that of J Elkington Gill. He had already, in collaboration with G P Manners, given the run-of-the-mill architecture of mid-nineteenth century Bath an added zest, for better or worse, at the Bluecoat School and even the Gas Works. The Convent of la Sainte Union [197] on Pulteney Road, now part of the City Magistrates' Court, displays the same awareness of contemporary trends. There is a solidity and massiveness about it reminiscent, perhaps, of William Butterfield's work of the 1850s although it is devoid of the polychromy. The front appears, at first glance, to be distressingly symmetrical, although closer examination shows this not so. The rear, however, now extended into new buildings, is looser and more carefully moulded: the stair turret is a particularly strong feature.

The same enthusiasm cannot be generated for the Royal School on Lansdown [198]. Built in 1856–8 by James Wilson as the Bath and Lansdown Proprietary College, it became the Royal School for the Daughters of Army Officers in 1865. There is no doubt that the building is asymmetrical but the arrangement and massing is so ill-considered that the effect is altogether unfortunate. Done in the Decorated style of the fourteenth century, the building really gives the appearance of a great jumble of architectural artefacts. The entrance is dominated by a four storey, heavily buttressed, square tower with a corner stair turret and spirelet and, cheek-by-jowl to this, is a tall gable end bearing a huge, ornate, oriel window. A rectangle and a triangle are placed side by side: neither wins and the result is confusion. Then, almost as if this centre piece is too much, the building spreads off in two relatively quiet wings, three storeys each and divided clearly into bays with simple, dormer windows. This building is what might be regarded as the work of a 'rogue' architect – one who paid little attention to current polemics and went his own way – such as Edward Buckton Lamb or Samuel Sanders Teulon. Their main characteristic was not so much simplicity, as Ruskin might have asked for, but confusion. Yet the best of them, as Teulon demonstrated only a few miles away at Tortworth Court, Gloucestershire (1849–51), had a fuller command of the style – Tortworth was almost Tudor, but Bestwood Lodge, Nottinghamshire (1862–4) was Decorated – and better control over their composition. Nevertheless, what is really most extraordinary about Wilson's design for the Royal School is how much it differs from his essay at Kingswood of five years earlier. What had happened to him in that short time?

If James Wilson's *forte* was not large Gothic schools, he did display a certain competence in Gothic villas. The early French Renaissance tower at Charlecombe Grove, with its noticeably Italian Gothic belvedere, has already been commented upon. Of similar scale but more distinctly Gothic were the additions proposed for The Beech [199] on Richmond Hill in 1869. The Beech was a handsome enough mid-Georgian house but clearly seen by the owner, Mr Evans, as being quite unfashionable. So a Gothic face lift was proposed: a new entrance tower with a belvedere and two hefty polygonal bay windows with deep machicolations below the parapet and a pointed dormer window above. The details throughout are copy-book Gothic. The porch doorway is pointed and heavily cusped, as are the twin windows of the belvedere. The frieze at both ground and first floor level is pierced with roundels which could well have become trefoils, and the paired windows of the bay and belvedere are separated by short, stumpy monial shafts with heavily carved capitals and bases. In accordance with the current desire for healthier living, all the window reveals are strongly splayed and plate glass is used in the sashes throughout, so as to admit the maximum of light.

It would be wrong to think that good High-Victorian Gothic was beyond the firm. The fresh input which William Willcox brought when he joined in 1866 generated, in 1867, at least one good High-Victorian Gothic house – eclectic, polychromatic and well handled – but it was at Trumpington near Cambridge. The market halls designed the next year for Abergavenny in Gwent demonstrated an ability, probably Willcox's again, for public buildings. And there are, hidden away in the lanes below Kingswood School, a number of quite convincing High-Victorian villas. Perhaps these are the work of Wilson and Willcox too.

199 The Beech, Richmond Hill, elevation In 1869 James Wilson employed carefully asymmetrical massing combined with familiar mediaeval detailing to convert a double-fronted Georgian house into a fashionable High Victorian villa.

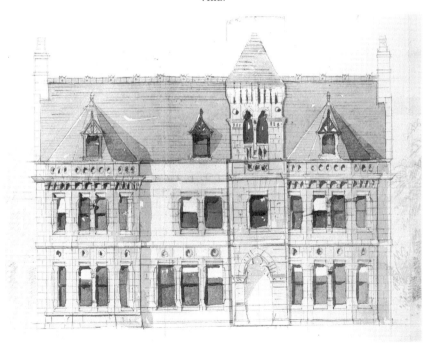

CHAPTER 7

Late-century Eclecticism

THE 'QUEEN ANNE' REVIVAL

In the mid-1860s faith in the Gothic as an architecture for the nineteenth century was fading. A number of the most talented younger Gothicists, men who had trained in the offices of Street and Scott in particular, began to doubt the sense in reviving a thirteenth-century style for nineteenth-century people to live in. The church building fever was beginning to abate and attention was now being turned towards other building types: houses and schools in particular. It was in these fields that the change in stylistic direction was first felt, and the innovators were Philip Speakman Webb, William Eden Nesfield, Edward Robert Robson, John James Stevenson and Richard Norman Shaw.

Almost at once these men rejected their Gothic masters and began to produce buildings of brilliant originality, and with total disregard for the rules: they fused Gothic planning and proportion with late-Renaissance details and homely materials. In effect they produced a style which was immediately appealing and represented a combination of all that was good in English architecture. These men were not afraid to borrow the smart white sash windows of Queen Anne and place them on an elevation boldly asymmetrical in the Gothic tradition, to hang their attics with plain tiles and decorate their eaves with Jacobean plasterwork, or curl their gables in the Dutch manner and arcade their façades as the architects of François Ier did. Their houses in the country tended to conform, early on, to what soon became known as the Old English style, but it was really in the towns that they made their mark. It was here that the style became the 'Queen Anne' Revival.

The 'Queen Anne' Revival was neither Queen Anne nor a revival. It was markedly original and about all that related to Queen Anne were the tall, thin, white-painted sash windows set in a red brick surround, within walls of yellow stock bricks. In this perhaps they did recall the Orangery at Kensington Palace, built in 1704. Following some highly original but strongly Gothic and proto-Arts and Crafts forays by Philip Webb – in the country the Red House at Bexleyheath, Kent (1859–60) and in town 14 Holland Park Road, London (1864–5) – the earliest and most unexpected Classical statement came from W Eden Nesfield in the Lodge he built at Kew Gardens, Surrey, in 1866–67. It is small, square and has a pyramidal roof with a massive central chimney which is its only possible Gothic feature. These buildings, however, were but a premonition of what was to come.

The year 1870 was important, socially, for the first Education Act. It is important, architecturally, for the same reason. Forster's Education Act required that primary schooling be provided for all children in the country – immediately. The result, particularly in London, was a school building programme on a scale which had never before been seen and has never since been equalled. Within the next twenty-five years some four hundred schools were built in the metropolis and they were largely the work of one man, E R Robson. The style chosen was neither Gothic, which was thought to relate to the established church, nor Classical, for this was seen as being non-conformist. It was mature Queen Anne Revival and, as such, had been introduced into London by Robson's then partner, J J Stevenson, in his own Red House on Bayswater Hill (1871). In addition to the features already noted there was now an even stronger Classical suggestion in the use of pediments and pilaster, keystones and cornices.

It was at this time that Norman Shaw, Nesfield's sometime partner, started building in London. Developing and urbanising the language of his Old English country houses of the 1860s, he produced a series of remarkable town houses including the present home of the Royal Geographical Society, Lowther Lodge, in Kensington Gore (1873–5), and one highly original office building, New Zealand Chambers (1871–73) in Leadenhall Street. In these buildings he achieved the feeling of Gothic without any of its trappings. The style thrived on its freedom and eclecticism and, appealing to the aesthetes amongst architects, it was widely published, for it made for good illustrations.

Possibly because Bath is a stone city and possibly because Bath already had a very well defined Classical framework for its domestic architecture, the Queen Anne Revival made little impression there. The most obvious use of red tile and white sash windows can be found in the suburban houses out along the Newbridge Road, or in the strangely confused Lansdown Grove Hotel where Old English gables are jumbled in with Mansard roofs and Jacobethan swags.

Yet there was one major building which, because of its prominence, drew attention to this style which other buildings in Bath seem to have passed by. This was Charles Edward Davis' Empire Hotel [200] of 1899–1901. Major Davis, as he was known, was the City Architect. The Empire Hotel was Bath's second largest purpose-built hotel, and building it in such a prominent and presumably valuable site would indicate an upswing in Bath's fortunes as a spa town. Its building closely followed the Pump Room Extension and was contemporaneous with the Guildhall Extension and the Victoria Art Gallery.

Throughout the country the first surge of hotel building which

200 The Empire Hotel, Parade Gardens and Bath Abbey Built by Charles Edward Davis in 1899–1901 and here photographed before the skyline was modified – compare this with [2] and [201] – the Empire Hotel and the Parade Gardens colonnade appear rich enough to upstage even the Abbey.

had followed in the wake of the railways was over and now a second wave of hotel building was under way. As the population became increasingly mobile and their requirements more sophisticated, a greater number of good hotels was needed: in London the top hotels were controlled by a Swiss who gave his name to the business, Cesar Ritz. It was Ritz who had Thomas Edward Collcutt build the Savoy in 1889 and then Sir Ernest George and Alfred Yeates rebuild Claridges in 1894–97. Meanwhile the first London hotel with bathrooms to every bedroom – the Carlton – was being built by the Bath-trained architect, Charles John Phipps, in 1891–99. The style of these hotels corresponds most closely to the domestic architecture introduced some twenty years earlier – the Queen Anne Revival. Thus there was adequate precedent for Davis' use of the style at the Empire Hotel.

What is most noticeable about the Empire Hotel is the heavily expressed balconied floors drawn, perhaps, from the chateaux of François Ier at Blois (1515–25) or Chambord (1519–47), which give the building a layered appearance. Although there are only five storeys below the great gables, there could have been seven or eight and the effect would be little different. In this the Empire Hotel is not unlike Collcutt's Savoy Hotel. By giving each storey an almost equal prominence, the capricious nature of the building is

201 The Empire Hotel, Dutch gable

clearly suggested. In the vertical plane, the building is suitably composed for the site. The corner is prominently expressed by the bolder detailing and the polygonal plan; the outside ends of the two facades are also set forward and, apparently heavier through the inclusion of bay windows, act as bookends to the mass of the building. The articulation is further stated in the varied roofline: triangular gables over the two end bays, an octagonal tower above the corner and broad, Dutch gables above the two recessed central bays. As a composition in masses the hotel works well enough but it is a challenge to the only other large building in the area, the Abbey.

So perhaps as a sop to the Abbey, the immediate impression of the hotel is of some sixteenth- or seventeenth-century concoction, a late but nevertheless approximate domestic counterpart of the church. The lower floors of the building are, architecturally, unified and display a blend of late-Mediaeval and early-Renaissance features – heavily mullioned and transomed windows set beside pilasters and pediments. The most ornate architecture appears at roof level where the Jacobethan corner tower, now devoid of much of its crowning stonework, was the

202 Worthington Road School, London
[201–202] The great brick gables of Edward Robert Robson's London Board schools provided a precedent for Charles Edward Davis' Empire Hotel of 1899: but they have since been rebuilt *sans* pilasters and pediment. See [200].

203 The Empire Hotel, ornamental and tile-hung gables

dominant feature. It was linked visually by the use of strongly expressed pilasters to the flanking Dutch gables. These have since been rebuilt [201] and so the original continuity breaks down. Yet they can still be seen as reflecting the London schools of Robson [202] and the ornate, gabled houses of the Queen Anne Revival. Consequently they play a part with the plastered and tile-hung triangular gables at the extremities [203] which themselves relate back, through heavily pargetted buildings like Shaw's New Zealand Chambers [204], to the Queen Anne Revival. It would seem likely that Alfred Holland, who commissioned the building, got good value for his £50,000. It is satisfying and yet rather ironic that, at the time of writing, the reversion of this building into a hotel is being contemplated.

When Davis was called in to build the Empire Hotel in 1899, he had just completed refacing the range of old houses and shops directly across the Orange Grove. These had avoided Georgian and early Victorian redevelopment and, in 1897, appeared much as they had done one hundred and sixty years earlier [205]. Davis, however, unified them [206], running the shop fronts through as a band at ground floor level and uniting all the gables into one long, ornamented, saw-tooth feature. He strengthened the previously

204 New Zealand Chambers, Leadenhall Street, London
[203–204] Ornamental plasterwork or pargetting, as used by Richard Norman Shaw in 1872 at New Zealand Chambers, added to the Picturesque roofline at Charles Edward Davis' Empire Hotel of 1899.

weak corner to Grand Parade by building it up as a tower with a balustrade and pyramid roof, and above each of the first floor windows he placed attractive shell-hoods, a motif he immediately repeated in the Dutch gables of the Empire Hotel. Probably because the existing walls were of irregular stone construction, the building was further unified with render and paint. And thus it presents a complete work, a combination of Classical decoration, Gothic form and finely worked details – consider the delicate, almost oriental arrangement of the window bars. This building, like its counterpart across the Orange Grove, could have happened at no other time.

ARTS AND CRAFTS ARCHITECTURE

While the architecture of Shaw and his generation moved inexorably towards Classicism, that of Shaw's pupils, men such as William Richard Lethaby and Edward Schroder Prior, continued on the eclectic trail. They heeded the words of William Morris, and sought to find a new, vernacular British architecture. Honesty and truthfulness, in structure and in form, was their tenet and in this

205 The Orange Grove before rebuilding

206 The Orange Grove

[205–206] Charles Edward Davis refaced the Orange Grove buildings in 1897, updating the gables and fenestration and adding a tower at the east end. The *ante* photograph [205] was taken c1894 from the scaffolding surrounding the new Guildhall extension.

they followed Pugin. They reacted against the nationalising effect of the industrial revolution, and sought to build within the local tradition, at a local level, in the vernacular. They saw architecture as a craft and as such associated it with the other crafts; metalwork, glasswork, woodwork, painting and tapestry. But above all they eschewed imitation and historicism and looked for originality.

Few examples of such work are readily found in Bath though many may lurk behind lush hedges on the surrounding hills. Yet just at the junction of Combe Park and Weston Lane there is a long, low building [207] which catches the eye. And it does so because it is different. It is definitely not Classical but then, not really Gothic, despite the heavily mullioned and transomed windows and the recessed arch in the centre. There is a sense of repose about it – its length and the wide splay of the eaves above the dormers and the porch – and a touch of sensuality in the slightly cusped eaves. And then there is something rather tactile and immediate about the materials – the plain tiles on the roof, now nicely mottled, and the chunky oakwork of the canopies above the doors. The stone, of course, is Bath stone, but that is the local building material. The building, four Memorial Cottages built in 1905, has a sense of belonging, of the vernacular.

It would be risible to say that public toilets have a sense of belonging. But there was little to offend about those which until recently stood on Marlborough Lane [208], just by the gates to the Royal Victoria Park, or the smaller building which still remains beneath the railway at North Parade Road and Pulteney Road. These must have been among the first public conveniences built in Bath and they were carried out with a dignity and style that belies their function. Once again the materials are simple and honest and the overall form, high level windows and a half-hipped roof with ventilation slits, is functional and to the point. The removal of the larger building to provide a new access route to the Charlotte Street car park deprived the city of a convenience probably greater than the convenience it sought to provide.

An appreciation of the need for healthy living – indeed, Bath's great function – was something often found in the domestic architecture of these years. Bathrooms became standard and many new houses were planned with a conscious awareness of the outside. Sir Edwin Lutyens' houses demonstrate this latter point well, whether it be the sleeping balcony at Monkton House, Sussex (1903) or the total integration of house and garden as at Deanery Garden, Berkshire (1899). One popular house plan which

was developed with the outside in mind was known as the
butterfly plan. Shaw had first used it in his Baroque rebuilding of

207 Memorial Cottages, Weston

208 Public toilets, Marlborough Lane

[207–208] Simplicity of form and honesty of construction characterize the
Memorial Cottages of 1905 and the public toilets which used to stand on
Marlborough Lane.

Chesters, Northumberland (1891), and his pupil Prior soon used it in a thoroughly Arts and Crafts manner at The Barn, Exmouth (1895–97). Here Arts and Crafts theory was taken to the extreme: the house was even faced with pebbles gathered from the beach. Such a plan offered many advantages. Firstly it combined formality with informality: while the formal segregation of the family wing and the service wing could be maintained, the informality of the butterfly plan, often accentuated in the silhouette of the building, could provide the required Picturesque and vernacular feel. And no longer had rooms to be placed to follow the course of the sun – morning room to the east and drawing room to the south west, and so on – the relatively linear form of the plan and its cranked arrangement provided a wider range of aspects for most rooms. Finally, there was the sun-trap, the terraced space between the arms of the building. One such house, Furze Hill, near Willersey in the Cotswolds, was built by J L Ball in 1912 with a double sun-trap on plan: not a single room faced north! Lawrence Weaver, writing in *Small Country Houses of Today* (1922), thought this planning to be 'strictly of today in its search for sunshine'.

A typical butterfly plan, with sun-trap overlooking the lush countryside towards Midford, can be seen at Ormidale on Southstoke Road [209, 210]. Built by T B Silcock and S S Reay c1910, this house is arranged with two wings set at 90° to each other with a cloistered terrace in between. The west wing holds the drawing room, and the east wing, the dining room. What is surprising, however, is the single storey scullery block reaching out to the north: careful planning could have avoided this. The materials used throughout are local – Bath stone in coursed rubble, stone tiles and oak woodwork. The design is simple and unadorned and what little expense is allowed is found in the coved panelling of the drawing room and the very Arts and Crafts oak stairs, boldly decorated with symbolic hearts: the home is where the heart is.

Very different, and really quite defensive in posture, is another house just along the ridge at Shaft Road, Combe Down. It was built in 1909, by one of the most important and idiosyncratic architects of this time: Charles Francis Annesley Voysey. The house was called Lodge Style [211] and deserves some consideration.

Unlike Voysey's other houses Lodge Style is neither roughcast nor whitewashed but it is no less a house in the 'Voysey Style'. It is a very strange building. It was built for T Sturge Cotterell who, so the story goes, wanted a house built in stone from his own quarry

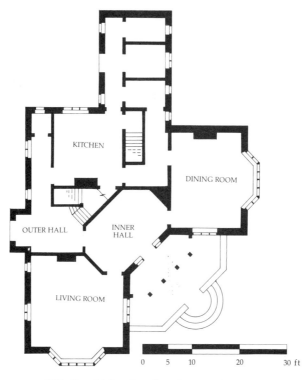

KITCHEN

DINING ROOM

OUTER HALL

INNER
HALL

LIVING ROOM

0   5   10   20   30 ft

209 Ormidale, Southstoke Road, plan

210 Ormidale, Southstoke Road

[209–210] By T B Silcock and S S Reay in c1910, Ormidale is in every way the comfortable, Arts and Crafts house. Built of local and homely materials, its butterfly plan fits snugly into the hillside yet the treatment of the servants' scullery at the rear remains rather unresolved.

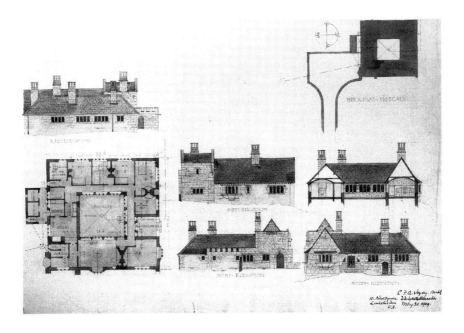

211 Lodge Style, Combe Down, plans and elevations

[211–212]Charles Francis Annesley Voysey built Lodge Style in 1909. Although constructed of Bath stone it owes little to the locality, its low profile and quadrangular form resulting from the 'peculiarities of the site, the building owner, and the purpose of the building'.

212 Lodge Style, Combe Down, preliminary design, plan

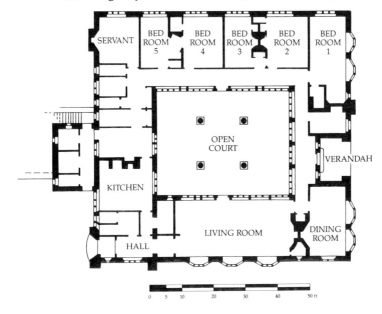

and reminiscent of Merton College, Oxford. In a way this is acceptable for, writing in *The Architectural Association Journal* in 1912, Voysey said that 'the important things in planning a house are the peculiarities of the site, the building owner, and the purpose of the building. It is from the consideration of these conditions alone that the finest architecture of the world has come'.

Two designs for the house were drawn up, the smaller one being built. Although essentially the same design, a single storey set around a central quadrangle, the original size of 80'6" by 72'9" [212] was reduced down to 59'6" by 57'0". The quadrangle shrank likewise and now it is a dank, rather unsuccessful open space in the centre of the house. Virtually the same arrangement of rooms was retained for the reduced scheme as had been proposed for the first. The building is entered at the north west corner, the entrance porch leading almost straight into the hall which runs along the length of the west side of the quadrangle. The drawing room, originally situated at the south west corner, is dispensed with in the smaller scheme, its function becoming that of the dining room, the hall reverting to its more mediaeval function as the focal point of the house, here interpreted as the living room. The south range is broken by a deep entrance porch, to the east of which are now the bedrooms which also run up the east side of the building. The north range is a collection of service rooms – box-room, bathroom, scullery and kitchen – opening once more onto the entrance lobby at the north west corner.

The dominant feature of the building is the entrance tower. It is here that what little ornament there is is located. 'Concentrated ornaments,' Voysey wrote, 'will help us towards making that ornament finer and more effective, as well as assisting towards the improvement in that quality generally'. Like Pugin, he believed that any decoration which was used should have a meaning. In the back of his mind he always held the Puginian dictum: 'There shall be no features about a building which are not necessary for convenience, construction and propriety.' Even the animal's head projecting from the tower was a gargoyle.

Pugin was of great importance to Voysey. To him he was a master, a 'truly devout individualist who designed to the best of his ability to meet the requirements and conditions which were presented to the mind . . . allowing his moral sentiments to play like a dancing light on every detail.' The Gothic details of the exterior of the house – the bay windows and the chimneys – are very reminiscent of Pugin's designs. Yet the use of Gothic detailing at Lodge Style has a greater significance than just the influence of Pugin. What could have been a design of thoroughly Classical symmeytry is asymmetrical in the extreme. 'We must clear our minds,' he wrote, 'of all conceptions of symmetrical elevations made after the likeness of temples, and return to the Gothic principles of evolving our homes out of local conditions and requirements'. The making of the plan subservient to the elevation, which itself was designed within predefined limits, was a thoroughly Classical idea, and to Voysey, unworthy of preoccupation.

> The Gothic process is the exact opposite; outside appearances are evolved from internal fundamental condition; staircases and windows come where most convenient to use. . . the creation of a beautiful Gothic building, instead of being a conception based on a temple made with hands, is based on the temple of a human soul.

It was a philosophy such as this which Philip Webb had first demonstrated in the house he built for William Morris at Bexleyheath back in 1859. And now, half a century later, the craftsmanship which Morris had championed was commonplace amongst architects. Surviving at the British Architectural Library is a drawing which could have been part of the first design for Lodge Style. It is, in fact, a tracing taken off Voysey's drawing for the gate at Broadleys, Windermere (1898), and it is a beautiful example of his abilities as a draughtsman. The gate was to be massive, with a vicious, dragon-headed catch of almost Scandinavian grotesqueness. As an example of a working drawing it is almost too fine: it is a piece of art in itself. And in this can be seen as much of Voysey the designer of wall papers and furniture as of Voysey the architect.

'FREE GOTHIC'

Although the use of Gothic detailing at Lodge Style was probably as much a result of the client's preoccupation with Merton College, Oxford, as anything, it was however noticeably contrary to the new century's growing interest in Classicism. For Shaw and his

213 Millbrook School, Widcombe, gables　C B Oliver's Millbrook School of
1902 has a lightness of touch and delicacy of detail which offsets the potentially
ponderous quality of the heavily fenestrated and gabled building.

circle had chosen to progress beyond the Queen Anne Revival
towards a Baroque derived from Vanbrugh and Wren. Yet Shaw's
slightly older contemporary, George Frederick Bodley, who had
come through Scott's office, maintained in his many churches a
path towards late-English Gothic. This was, in its way, as much a
reaction against the Decorated dogma of the High-Victorian
Gothic as Shaw's Old English and Queen Anne Revival had been,
for the Perpendicular and the Tudor had been derided by Pugin
and rejected by his disciples. Although reserved mainly for
ecclesiastical work, Bodley's form of Gothic was very influential
and its presence can be seen in Sir Thomas Graham Jackson's
Memorial Cloister at Bath Abbey in 1923 [157].

It was Jackson who, in his building of the Oxford Examination
Schools in 1876, had brought the 1830s interest in Tudor,
Elizabethan and Jacobean architecture full circle and had given
these late-Gothic and early-Renaissance styles new respectability
in the secular context. In time, the distinctly Tudor forms of
expressed gables and heavily mullioned and transomed windows
were picked up and fused with the more free and vernacular forms
associated with the Arts and Crafts. It was another case of
nationalism.

In Bath this 'free Gothic' can be discovered near the foot of Lyncombe Hill at Millbrook School [213], built in 1902 by C B Oliver, the designer of the Town Hall at Calne. Stylistically the building is Tudor and conventional enough: large mullioned and transomed windows set in two matching gables. But it is the details between these windows that catch the eye and speak of the Arts and Crafts and a new spirit of freedom. Set in the centre of the

214 St Michael's Church House, Walcot Street

215 St Michael's Church House, Walcot Street, doorway
[214–215] Built in 1904 by Wallace Gill, St Michael's Church House displays fine
craftsmanship in both the decoration and the detailing.

216 Claverton Down Gospel Hall, Claverton Down Road T B Silcock and S S Reay's Gospel Hall of 1896–97 is, despite its exquisite sculpture, a disarmingly simple building.

symmetrical elevation is a deep hood, sheltering an exquisite wrought-iron bell. The lines of the stone parapet between the gables above and on the balcony below play convex forms against concave. From the roof the rainwater drains through an ornamental lead hopper-head bearing the date, and crowning this composition is a square cupola. Set askance the ridge, it is of a delicacy comparable to fine furniture and confirms the sensitivity to craftsmanship already suggested.

Another building of equally delicate form is St Michael's Church House on Walcot Street [214]. It was built in 1904 by Wallace Gill, the son of J Elkington Gill, and was described at the time as 'a handsome building, having a picturesque front with mullioned windows'. But there was more to it than that. There is a feeling of fine craftmanship in the delicate bellcote and spire, and in the eponymous figure of St Michael above the door [215]. This sculpture serves to hold together the open pediment of the doorway and the stepped windows above: without the sculpture the façade would be hollow. This strange composition, and its detail – in particular the lettering over the door – is as close to *Art Nouveau* as can be found in Bath. And, frankly, that is not very close.

Equally intriguing and no less unlikely in Bath, is T B Silcock's

Claverton Down Gospel Hall [216] of 1896–7. It is not so much the Voyseyesque render and buttressing which here catch the eye, but the quite beautiful angels kneeling on the corners of the gables. It is surprising that this came from the same office as the ponderous YMCA building in Broad Street (1887). Despite being mayor of Bath twice, Silcock maintained a busy practice with his partner S S Reay, and it was Reay who designed the neat, bronze, Classical panels which now draw attention to famous residences through-out Bath.

'FREE CLASSIC'

Major Davis had been elected a Fellow of the Society of Antiquaries as a very young man in 1850, and it was his interest in archaeology which led to the eventual extension of the Pump Room and the rebuilding of the Baths. In 1869 Davis discovered and exposed extensive Roman thermal works at the Baths which, although known of for many years, had never been explored. In 1877 he exposed the Roman well beneath the King's Bath and in 1880 discovered the Great Bath and four years later, the Circular Bath, also Roman remains. The Corporation, realising the potential of these discoveries, sent Davis to Baden-Baden and Karlsbad in 1885 on a fact finding mission with the eventual aim of re-establishing Bath as a leading spa town. As a result, Davis became an expert on thermal baths and was consulted by the Corporations of Harrogate and Droitwich.

Davis began to rebuild the Old Baths in 1885, demolishing the Queen's Bath (built in 1597, and later named after Anne, wife of James I), as well as Baldwin's work on the south end of the Pump Room colonnade. Davis' replacement was extravagent and richly Classical: one contemporary critic saw the designs as saturated with the grossness of the German Renaissance. The bridge over York Street and the ornate Laundry chimney yet remain. But in 1886 Davis ran into trouble when part of the new works collapsed and a workman was killed. At the inquest the contractor was exonerated of blame and thus the verdict went against the City Architect. Meanwhile, the Society of Antiquities took Davis to task on archaeological as well as structural grounds. In 1887 arbitration was sought from Alfred Waterhouse, architect of the National History Museum and president-elect of the Royal Institute of British Architects, who found Davis' new work to be structurally sound, although of slender construction, and altogether a careful compromise between the utility of the Baths and their archaeological value. Yet the Corporation's faith in their Architect must have been shaken by this near débâcle and when it was decided to extend the Guildhall in 1891 an open competition was offered from which Davis was excluded.

In 1891 the Bath City Magistrates had passed a resolution which brought to the Council's attention the need for a better Court. Baldwin's building of 1776 could no longer cope with the increased requirements of a small but busy Victorian city, so the Council sought the advice of William Young, a Scottish architect then working in London. Young had recently completed the Municipal Chambers in Glasgow (1883–88), a building whose grand civic gesture must have impressed the Councillors of Bath. Young recommended the retention of Baldwin's Guildhall and suggested two options: either the addition of side wings to the old building or the erection of a new block to extend along the whole length of Bridge Street to the north. The first option was chosen and the city announced the competition which called for designs to provide new Municipal Offices and, in accordance with a recent government directive, a Technical School.

In response to the call, nineteen competition entries were received and three selected. Two Bath architects, T B Silcock, and Messrs Burges and Oliver came third and second respectively, but the first place was taken by a London architect, John McKean Brydon. Like Young, Brydon was a Scot and he had worked as assistant to Shaw and Nesfield. Now well established – he had recently completed the Chelsea Town Hall (1885–87) – Brydon was able, at Bath, to try out the Vanbrughesque Baroque which was to serve him well a few years later when he received the major commission for the new Government Offices on Parliament Square (1898–1912). It is interesting to note that the War Office in Whitehall, the other big public commission of 1898, went to William Young: one could speculate on how well those two London-Scots knew each other.

Brydon's scheme centred on Baldwin's Guildhall [217, 218]. To the north he put the Technical School and to the south, linked by an arched screen to Davis' Police Station, the Municipal Offices. From the centre he extended the architectural language of Baldwin's elevation outwards, picking up lines of the heavily rusticated base and of the pedimented windows. Where the building rounded the corners to north and south, the recessed

217 The Guildhall

outer windows and Giant Order columns of Baldwin's elevation were repeated. But here Brydon also allowed himself some freedom. To the porches he gave banded columns, and to the skyline two great voluted and arcaded cupolas [219]. Such Baroque features would usually be traced back to Vanbrugh: see again Blenheim or Castle Howard. But now, in 1893, the direct inspiration was far more recent. The clue to what Brydon must have been looking at lies in the curious friezes set high up between the Giant Order columns on the rounded corners of the building. There was only one building which could have suggested this treatment to Brydon: this was the Institute of Chartered Accountants [220], off Moorgate, in London. Designed by John Belcher and Arthur Beresford Pite in 1888 it was, at the time of the Bath competition, still being built. Yet its effect on Brydon's design was considerable and should remove the latter from the obscurity in which it has languished too long.

In turn-of-the-century London, John Belcher's office was as much sought after as those of Shaw, Sir Ernest George and Sir Aston Webb. A Royal Academician, Royal Gold Medalist and President of the Royal Institute of British Architects, his contribution to the architecture of that time was immense, but has been little appreciated. When in 1884 E S Prior and another of

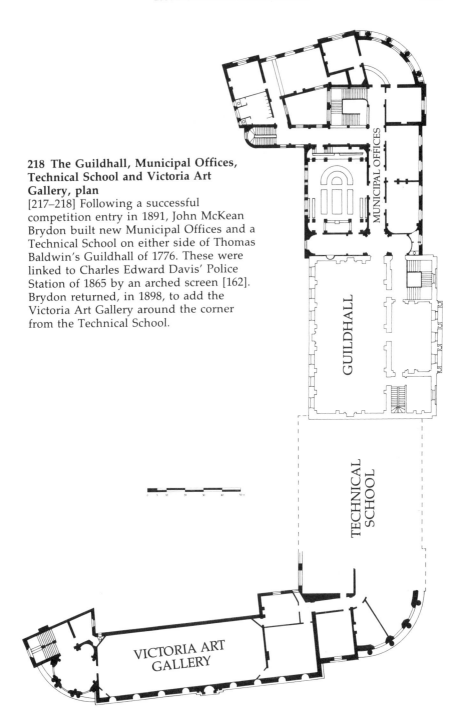

218 The Guildhall, Municipal Offices, Technical School and Victoria Art Gallery, plan
[217–218] Following a successful competition entry in 1891, John McKean Brydon built new Municipal Offices and a Technical School on either side of Thomas Baldwin's Guildhall of 1776. These were linked to Charles Edward Davis' Police Station of 1865 by an arched screen [162]. Brydon returned, in 1898, to add the Victoria Art Gallery around the corner from the Technical School.

219 The Guildhall, cupola

220 The Institute of Chartered Accountants, off Moorgate, London
[219–220] In his Guildhall Extension, begun in 1893, John McKean Brydon
employed heavy English Baroque detailing reminiscent of Sir Christopher
Wren or, perhaps, Sir John Vanbrugh. See [76]. The plastic nature of the
Baroque had recently been exposed by John Belcher and Arthur Beresford Pite
at the Institute of Chartered Accountants of 1888. This architecture became
known as Arts and Crafts Baroque.

221 Institute of Chartered Accountants, off Moorgate, London, ornamental
frieze

222 Technical School, ornamental frieze

Shaw's pupils, W R Lethaby, founded the Art Worker's Guild, it was Belcher whom they chose as chairman of the first meeting. The Guild was set up, in a mediaeval manner, to reverse 'the drifting apart of the arts of architecture, painting and sculpture'. It was just such an integration which Belcher and Pite, another founder member of the Guild, demonstrated four years later at the Institute of Chartered Accountants. The plastic nature of Baroque made it the most natural style for this fusion, for here, painting and sculpture could become part of the architecture in a way rarely achieved in other styles, even in Gothic. This Vanbrughesque style became known, because of its combination of disciplines and touches of individuality and Classical language, as Arts and Crafts Baroque.

The Baroque of the Institute of Chartered Accountants was widely copied – by Thomas Collcutt, for instance, at Lloyds Shipping Register in London (1900) – but nowhere as soon as at Brydon's Guildhall Extension at Bath. The banded columns and arcaded cupola already observed can be traced, like the frieze, back to Belcher. At the Institute of Chartered Accountants, Belcher had used the frieze [221], cut by Hamo Thorneycroft, to represent

223 Municipal Offices, ornamental frieze
[221–223] Hamo Thornycroft's ornamental frieze at the Institute of Chartered Accountants became the model for G A Lawson's rather more Stoic interpretation at the Guildhall Extension. See *Appendix 1*.

the fields associated with the institute. Brydon did the same at Bath where G A Lawson's figures at the north corner depict the subjects taught at the Technical School [222] and those on the south, the aspirations of the Judiciary and Corporation of the city [223] (See also Appendix 1).

The foundation stone for the Guildhall Extension was laid amid much ceremony on 1 June 1893. Although the tenders had been received nine months earlier, that of Messrs Haywood and Wooster being accepted, the building had been delayed due to complaints that it was too near the Abbey and too large for the High Street. As a result the design was changed, the wings being set back and both the length and accommodation reduced. The result was a building less impressive than had been envisaged but, nonetheless, proud.

Before moving on to Brydon's second major work in Bath, a word should be said of his third and final building, the Art Gallery and Library. Built in 1898 as a memorial to the Queen's Diamond Jubilee, the Victoria Art Gallery picked up the style of the adjacent Technical School and carried it on, rusticated and balustraded, down the length of Bridge street [218]. At the corner with Grand Parade, Brydon placed the entrance vestibule and topped it with a dome. In contrast to the ornate Corinthian of the earlier building, the order here was Doric. The now unused entrance in the Bridge Street façade provided access to the Reference and Guildhall Library and the niched figure above, in the centre of the powerful blank wall of the first floor picture gallery, was Queen Victoria. The statues intended for the other eight niches never materialised.

Brydon's second major building in Bath was again the result of a competition, the Pump Room Extension. Held in 1894, this competition sought designs for an enclosure to the Great Bath and the provision of a concert room. Brydon's winning design [224] was based on the same approach he had used at the Guildhall – a matching extension of the existing building. Here at the Baths, he extended the elevation of Baldwin's Pump Room towards the Abbey, running the string courses and balustrade through and building a second, matching portico. Behind this was the huge domed concert hall and beyond that the Great Bath, covered with a typically Roman thermae building. This design, like so many other winning designs in nineteenth-century architectural competitions, was not built.

Brydon was lucky, for he was able to redesign the building in what, presumably, was a far cheaper form, and to retain the

224 The Pump Room Ballroom, winning competition entry

225 The Pump Room Ballroom   John McKean Brydon's winning entry for the 1894 Pump Room Ballroom competition was not built. In the event he redesigned and built his scheme in a more muted, Palladian manner.

commission. The Great Bath lost its covering, the concert hall was reduced in size and the dome diminished drastically. The new design [225] was no longer an extension of Baldwin's Pump Room but a separate building in an earlier Palladian manner, connected by a low linking block. Although it lacked some of the scale of the first design, it was more honest, allowing the concert hall to stand on its own.

The single storey wall which formed the link to the Pump Room was continued, beyond the concert hall, right around the Great Bath. Behind this was the open arcade which surrounded the sunken Baths in a manner similar to Brydon's original conception. In place of the roof there appeared the now well-known statues of eight Roman emperors and generals, all of whom were engaged in the conquest and occupation of ancient Britain. Here again Brydon used the sculptor G A Lawson. (See also Appendix 2). This whole Roman composition was overlooked by a great Diocletian window beneath the pedimented end wall of the concert hall. And it is here, inside, that Brydon moves away from Palladian or Roman architecture to something, once again, more Baroque. The splendour of the concert hall is its great, domed ceiling. The suitable references to Roman ceilings are there, in the coffered, barrel vault at either end of the hall, but more interesting really is that the decoration of the dome itself comes straight from Wren's church of St Stephen Walbrook: this is pure Wrennaisance.

One other important London architect came to work in Bath in the Classical manner, Sir Reginald Blomfield, and he rebuilt the

226 The Pulteney Hotel, Sydney Gardens

227 The Holborne of Menstrie Museum, formerly the Pulteney Hotel, Sydney Gardens [226–227] The old Sydney Hotel had been built by Charles Harcourt Masters in 1794–95 and in 1836 it had received an attic storey from the younger John Pinch. Renamed the Pulteney Hotel, it had been purchased in 1910 by the trustees of the Holborn of Menstrie Museum for whom Sir Reginald Blomfield gutted, refaced and Francofied the building in 1913–16.

Holbourne of Menstrie Museum in 1913–1916. He had been articled to his uncle, Sir Arthur Blomfield, architect of St John the Baptist, in 1881, and although initially drawn towards the Arts and Crafts circle of Prior and Lethaby, he eventually emerged as a champion of Classicism, the Beaux Arts tradition, and an expert on French architecture, in particular that of the eighteenth century and Louis XV. He published his masterly *History of French Architecture* in four volumes in 1911 and 1921 and while working on the Holbourne of Menstrie Museum he was President of the Royal Institute of British Architects, and recipient in 1913 of the Royal Gold Medal. Yet the Holbourne is rather disappointing.

The original building had been altered long before, in 1836, by the younger John Pinch, who added an awkward attic storey to the three-storey building [226]. By 1910, when it was purchased by the Trustees of the Museum, it was empty and derelict. It was regarded as 'a typical example of the very late Georgian manner, when refinement and restraint had continued to produce rather dull and uninteresting architecture.' The proportions were, admittedly, peculiar: the *piano nobile* windows were too long and the rusticated *piano rustica* was too shallow, this being accentuated by the arcade and the long side wings. Yet the critic of the building was perhaps a little too poetic in his appreciation of Blomfield's work [227]. The description continues:

> In Sir Reginald Blomfield's restoration there is a marked difference. The building possesses a subtle flavour of romance, a sort of aspiration and mystery, which are totally lacking in the original. We are reminded slightly of Vanbrugh by this design; but, needless to say, the detail has none of his atrocious coarseness. There is unquestionably the sensation of a living creation here; one could easily believe that it belongs to an earlier age.

What Blomfield actually did to the outside was largely governed by his treatment of the interior, which he virtually gutted. He cast the first and second floor as one space, the museum, and turned the attic storey into the top-lit picture gallery. Thus he could do away with the row of square mezzanine windows below the cornice which had served the second floor, and also those above the pediment in the attic, as it was now top-lit.

Outside, the extending side wings were removed and replaced by a colonnade, and the number of windows in the *piano rustica* reduced. This made the base appear heavier and more in proportion, and gave the central arcade some greater dignity. Above this the *piano nobile* windows were set in a panel decorated with swags and medallions with the effect of attenuating the windows, so that they could no longer dominate those of the now strengthened base. In this the recast façade recalls Jacques-Ange Gabriel's angle pavilions in the Place de la Concorde in Paris (1753–70). Finally, the composition was set off with a balustrade and urns on the skyline, with the effect of lightening Pinch's rather heavy attic.

So far Blomfield's work appears quite acceptable and would have been better had the double colonnade originally intended for each side been carried out. What was built was possibly derived from Emmanuel Héré de Corny's Hemicycle at the Place du Gouvernement at Nancy (1750–57). But go behind the building and view the rear. It appears over fenestrated, particularly at ground floor, and is dominated by an upstanding central bay, lighting the stairs, which serves to split the composition right down the centre. Blomfield's skill in readdressing the proportions of the front have here gone quite to waste.

EPILOGUE

If it was Sir Thomas Graham Jackson's Memorial Cloister at Bath Abbey which provided, in 1923, the city's final Gothic gesture, it was Sir Reginald Blomfield, his old companion-in-arms in the heated debate on whether architecture was a profession or an art, who might have had the last word in the Classical language. Blomfield, architect of the Menin Gate and designer of the Great War Cross, built the city's memorial to the dead of the Great War at Queen's Parade, just outside the Rivers Gate, in 1926.

Dead styles, one might now think, for dead men: for in those middle years of the 1920s the Modern Movement, a new architecture for a new world, was unveiled. But if the memory of the dead has faded in these last seventy years, the architecture with which the city of Bath remembered them certainly has not. With just a shudder during the rapacious years of the 1960s, twentieth-century Bath slid from Free Classic to Neo-Georgian to Post-Modern Classicism, and building in the city now thrives in a way hardly matched since the last decade of the nineteenth century. In Bath, it is as if the Modern Movement never happened at all or, if it did, it got lost in a storm of light yellow sandstone.

APPENDIX ONE

The Municipal Buildings and Technical School, Bath

Architect: John McKean Brydon   Sculptor: G A Lawson

Figures in frieze (not in order of place)

1 North end, left hand panel
   Electricity, Applied Electricity, Navigation, Building, Physics, Chemistry, Engineering

2 North end, centre panel
   Minerva, Poetry, Astronomy, Tragedy, Comedy, Agriculture, Women's Industry

3 North end, right hand panel
   Architecture, Painting, Sculpture, Music, Poetry, Woodcarving, Metalwork

4 South end, left hand panel
   Justice and Mercy, Protection (2 figures), Light of Learning, Order, Law

5 South end, centre panel
   'City of Bath' (centre), 'The genii of the healing waters' (seated), Commerce (right), Industry (left), Justice and Truth, Temple of Minerva (in background)

6 South end, right hand panel
   Education (2 figures), Hospitality (2 figures), Recreation (2 figures)

APPENDIX TWO

The Pump Room Extension, Bath

Architect: John McKean Brydon   Sculptor: G A Lawson

Figures around the Great Bath

Emperors   Julius Caesar
             Claudius
             Hadrian
             Constantine the Great
             Vespian

Generals   Ostorius
             Scapula (who defeated Caractacus)
             Seutonius Paulinus (who defeated Boadicea)
             Agricola

BIBLIOGRAPHY

1. Bath and the counties of Somerset and Avon

anon, *A Brief Account of the Proceedings Relative to the Formation of the Royal Victoria Park with the First Report of the Committee*, Bath, 1831

Bath Abbey Church Restoration Committee, *Annual Report*, Bath, 1865–72

Bishop, Philippa, 'Beckford in Bath', *Bath History*, vol ii, 1988

Brereton, R P, *Somerset Church Towers*, c1904

Carter, John, *Some Account of the Abbey Church at Bath*, London, 1798

Clarke, Gillian, *Prior Park: A Compleat Landscape*, Bath, 1987

Crallan, Hugh, 'Beckford in Bath', *Architectural Review*, March 1968

Cunliffe, Barry, 'Major Davis: Architect and Antiquarian', *Bath History*, vol i, 1986

Davis, Charles E, *The Mineral Baths of Bath*, Bath, 1883

Ellison, Fred E, *Etchings of Bath*, London, 1888

Harris, John, 'C R Cockerell's "Ichnographica Domestica" ', *Architectural History*, vol 14, 1971

Hill, Mary K, *Bath and the Eighteenth Century Novel*, Bath, 1989

Irvine, J T, *Description of the Remains of the Norman Cathedral of Bath, Exposed During the Repairs Made Between 1863 and 1872*, Bath, 1890

Ison, Walter, *The Georgian Buildings of Bath from 1700 to 1830*, Bath, 1948

Jackson, Thomas Graham, *Report on Exterior Masonry and Sculpture, Bath Abbey*, Bath, 1899

Lansdown, H V, *Recollections of the Late William Beckford*, Bath, 1893

Lees-Milne, James and David Ford, *Images of Bath*, Richmond-upon-Thames, 1982

Little, Bryan, *The Buildings of Bath 47–1947*, London, 1947

McBryde, William *et al*, *Beyond Mr Pulteney's Bridge*, Bath, 1987

McLaughlin, David; Rosemary Northcote and Julian Orbach, *Victorian Bath*, Bath, 1979

Meehan, J F, *Famous Houses of Bath and District*, Bath, 1901

Meehan, J F, *More Famous Houses of Bath and District*, Bath, 1906

Millington, Jon, *Beckford's Tower, Bath*, Bath, 1983

Mowl, Tim, 'A Taste for Towers', *Country Life*, 1 October 1987

Mowl, Tim, 'The Williamane – Architecture for the Sailor King', in Roger

White and Caroline Lightburn (eds.), *Late Georgian Classicism*, London, 1988

Mowl, Tim and Brian Earnshaw, *John Wood, Architect of Obsession*, Bath, 1988

Murch, Jerome, *Biographical Sketches of Bath Celebrities*, London and Bath, 1893

Neale, R S, *Bath 1680–1850: A Social History*, London, Boston and Henley, 1981

Page, William (ed), *The Victorian History of Somerset*, vol ii, London, 1911

Peach, R E, *Historic Houses in Bath*, vol i, London 1883

Peach, R E, *Historic Houses in Bath*, vol ii, London, 1884

Peach, R E, *Street-lore of Bath*, London, 1893

Pensley, B, *The Bath Pump Room Competition: Its Rise and Fall*, Bath, 1894

Pevsner, Nikolaus, *The Buildings of England, North Somerset and Bristol*, Harmondsworth, 1958

Pevsner, Nikolaus, *The Buildings of England, South and West Somerset*, Harmondsworth, 1958

Pound, Christopher, *Genius of Bath: The City and Its Landscape*, Bath, 1986

Poyntz Wright, Peter, *The Parish Church Towers of Somerset 1350–1550*, Amersham, 1980

Prentis, Rev Richard, *The Parish Church of St Mary the Virgin, Bathwick*, *Bath*, Bath, 1973

Robertson, Charles, *Bath, an Architectural Guide*, London, 1975

Scott, Maurice, *Discovering Widcombe and Lyncombe: A Short History of These Two Parishes of Bath*, Bath, 1984

Stone, Barbara G, *Bath Millenium: the Christian Movement 973–1973*, Bath, nd

Summers, Peter and Phillipa Bishop, *William Beckford, Some Notes on his Life in Bath 1822–1844*, London, 1966

Tobin, P F J, *Prior Park College, Chapel of Our Lady of the Snows, a Centenary History*, Bath, 1982

Walter, Tony, 'The Decline of the Georgian Terrace', *Period Home*, January 1985

Webster, Christopher, 'The Influence of John Soane' in Roger White and Caroline Lightburn (eds.), *Late Georgian Classicism*, London, 1988

Williams, J Anthony, *Bath and Rome: the Living Link*, Bath, 1963

Wood, John, *A Description of Bath*, London, 1765; Bath, 1969

Wriston, Barbara, *Rare Doings at Bath*, Chicago, 1978

2.   Books cited in the text

Adam, Robert, *The Ruins of the Palace of the Emperor Diocletian at Spalatro in Dalmatia*, 1764

Adam, Robert and James, *The Works in Architecture of Robert and James Adam*, London, 1773 ff

Austen, Jane, *Northanger Abbey*, London, 1818

Blomfield, Sir Reginald, *A History of French Architecture*, London, 1911, 1921

Bourne, John C, *History and Description of the Great Western Railway*, London, 1846

Boyle, Richard (Lord Burlington), *Fabbriche Antiche Disegnate da Andrea Palladio*, London, 1730

Britton, John, *The Architectural Antiquities of Great Britain*, London, 1807–35

Britton, John, *Cathedral Antiquities of England*, London, 1814–35, 1836

Campbell, Colen, *Vitruvius Britannicus*, vols i–iii, London, 1717–25, 1731

Chambers, William, *A Treatise on Civil Architecture*, London, 1759

Chambers, William, *The Gardens and Buildings of Kew*, London, 1763

Clarke, Thomas Hutchings, *Domestic Architecture of the Reigns of Queen Elizabeth and James I*, London, 1833

Cottingham, Lewis Nockalls, *Ornamental Metalworkers Director*, London, 1823

Disraeli, Benjamin, *Contarini Fleming*, London, 1832

Eastlake, Charles L, *A History of the Gothic Revival*, London, 1872

English, Edward, *Views of Lansdown Tower*, London, 1844

Ferrey, Benjamin, *Recollections of A N Welby Pugin and His Father Augustus Pugin*, London, 1861

Gandy, Joseph Michael, *Designs for Cottages, Farms and other Rural Buildings*, London, 1805

Gandy, Joseph Michael, *The Rural Architect*, London, 1805

Gibbs, James, *A Book of Architecture*, London, 1728

Hamilton, George Ernest, *Designs for Rural Churches*, London, 1837

Hope, Thomas, *Observations on the Plan and Elevations . . . for Downing College, Cambridge, in a letter to Francis Annesley esq. MP by Thomas Hope*, 1804

Hunt, Thomas Frederick, *Exemplars of Tudor Architecture Adapted to Modern Habitations*, London, 1830

Inwood, Henry William, *The Erectheion: Fragments of Athenian Architecture and a Few Remains in Attica, Megara and Epirus*, London, 1827

Jackson, John George, *Designs for Villas*, London, 1828

Jackson, Thomas Graham, *Modern Gothic Architecture*, London, 1873

Jackson, Thomas Graham, *Reason in Architecture*, London, 1906

Kelsall, Charles, *Phantasm of a University*, London, 1814

Knight, Henry Gally, *The Ecclesiastical Architecture of Italy from the Time of Constantine to the 15th Century*, London, 1842–44

Knight, Henry Gally, *Saracenic and Norman Remains to Illustrate the Normans in Sicily*, London, 1838

Knight, Richard Payne, *The Landscape, a Didactic Poem*, London, 1794

Langley, Batty, *City and County Builder's and Workman's Treasury of Designs*, London, 1740

Langley, Batty and Thomas Langley, *Gothic Architecture, Improved. . .*, London, 1747

Loudon, John Claudius, *Encyclopedia of Cottage, Farm and Villa Architecture*, London, 1833

Loudon, John Claudius, *The Gardener' Magazine*, London, 1843 ff

Loudon, John Claudius, *On The Laying Out, Planting and Managing of Cemetries, and on the Improvement of Churchyards*, London 1843

Lugar, Robert, *Architectural Sketches for Cottages, Rural Dwellings and Villas*, London, 1805

Nash, Joseph, *The Mansions of England in the Olden Times*, London, 1839–49

Pain, William, *The Practical House Carpenter*, London, 1805

Papworth, John Buonarotti, *Rural Residences*, London, 1818, 1832

Parker, Charles, *Villa Rustica*, London, 1832–41

Price, Uvedale, *Essay on the Picturesque*, London, 1794

Pugin, A Welby, *An Apology for the Revival of Christian Architecture*, London, 1843

Pugin, A Welby, *Contrasts*, Salisbury, 1836; London, 1841

Pugin, A Welby, *The True Principles of Pointed or Christian Architecture*, London, 1841

Repton, Humphrey, *Sketches and Hints on Landscape Gardening*, London, 1794

Revett, Nicholas, *Ionian Antiquities*, London, 1769, 1797

Richardson, Charles, James, *Observations on the Architecture of England During the Reigns of Queen Elizabeth and James I*, London, 1837

Robinson, Peter Frederick, *Designs for Ornamental Villas*, London, 1825–27

Robinson, Peter Frederick, *Rural Architecture, or a Series of Designs for Ornamental Cottages*, London, 1823

Ruskin, John, *Lectures on Architecture and Painting*, Orpington, 1853

Ruskin, John, *The Seven Lamps of Architecture*, Orpington, 1849

Ruskin, John, *The Stones of Venice*, vol i, Orpington, 1851

Ruskin, John, *The Stones of Venice*, vols ii and iii, Orpington, 1853

Scott, George Gilbert, *Lectures on the Rise and Development of Mediaeval Architecture*, London, 1879

Scott, George Gilbert, *Remarks on Secular and Domestic Architecture Present and Future*, London, 1858

Shaw, Henry, *Details of Elizabethan Architecture*, London, 1839

Shepherd, Thomas H, *Metropolitan Improvements or London in the Nineteenth Century*, London, 1829

Smollett, Tobias, *The Expedition of Humphry Clinker*, London, 1771

Street, George Edmund, *Brick and Marble Architecture, Notes of a Tour in the North of Italy*, London, 1855

Stuart, James and Nicholas Revett, *The Antiquities of Athens*, London, 1762 ff

Taylor, George Ledwell and Edward Cresy, *The Architectural Antiquities of Rome*, London, 1821–22

Viollet-le-Duc, Eugene, *Entretiens Sur l'Architecture*, Paris, 1863–72

Vitruvius, *De Architectura Libri Decem (Ten Books on Architecture)*

Ware, Issac, *A Complete Body of Architecture*, London, 1756

Weaver, Lawrence, *Small Country Houses of Today*, London, 1922
Wetten, Robert, *Designs for Villas in the Italian Style of Architecture*, London, 1830
Wilkins, William, *Antiquities of Magna Graecia*, Cambridge, 1807
Wilkins, William, *Atheniensia*, London, 1816
Wilkins, William, *Civil Architecture of Vitruvius*, London, 1813, 1817
Wilkins, William, *Prolusiones Architectonicae*, London, 1837
Woolfe, John and Gandon, James, *Vitruvius Britannius*, vol iv, London, 1767

3. Newspapers and journals cited in the text

The Architectural Association Journal
The Athenaeum
The Bath and West Evening Chronicle
The Bath and Country Gazette
The Builder
The Ecclesiologist
The Mirror of Literature, Amusement and Instruction
The Observer
Transactions of the Royal Institute of British Architects

4. General reference material

Bond, Francis, *Gothic Architecture in England*, London, 1912
Clarke, B F L, *Church Builders of the Nineteenth Century*, Newton Abbot, 1969
Clark, Kenneth, *The Gothic Revival*, London, 1962
Cobb, Gerald, *English Cathedrals, the Forgotten Centuries*, London, 1980
Colvin, Howard, *A Biographical Dictionary of British Architects 1600–1840*, London, 1978
Crook, J Mordaunt, *The Greek Revival*, London, 1972
Davey, Peter, *Arts and Crafts Architecture: the Search for Earthly Paradise*, London, 1980
Dixon, Roger and Stefan Muthesius, *Victorian Architecture*, London, 1978
Downes, Kerry, *Vanbrugh*, London, 1978
Fellows, Richard A, *Sir Reginald Blomfield: An Edwardian Architect*, London, 1985
Fletcher, Sir Banister, *A History of Architecture on the Comparative Method*, London, 1963

Gebhard, David, *Charles F A Voysey, Architect*, Los Angeles, 1975

Girouard, Mark, 'Attitudes to Elizabethan Architecture, 1600–1900' in John Summerson (ed), *Concerning Architecture*, London, 1968

Girouard, Mark, *Sweetness and Light: the 'Queen Anne' Movement 1860–1900*, Oxford, 1977

Gloag, John, *Mr Loudon's England*, Newcastle-upon-Tyne, 1970

Hitchcock, Henry-Russell, *Early Victorian Architecture in Britain*, London, 1972

Hussey, Christopher, *The Picturesque*, London, 1927

Kornwolf, James D, *M H Baillie Scott and the Arts and Crafts Movement*, Baltimore and London, 1972

Liscombe, R W, *William Wilkins*, Cambridge, 1980

Lukacher, Brian *et al*, *Joseph Michael Gandy 1771–1843*, London, 1982

Mackintosh, Ian and Michael Sell (eds), *Curtains or a New Life for Old Theatres*, London, 1982

Meller, Hugh, *London Cemeteries*, Amersham, 1981

Middleton, Robin and David Watkin, *Neo Classical and 19th Century Architecture*, New York, 1980

Muthesius, Stefan, *The High Victorian Movement in Architecture 1850–1870*, London and Boston, 1972

Piranesi, Francesco, *Vues de Differentes Trois Grands Edifices*, Roma, 17--

Pevsner, Nikolaus, *Some Architectural Writers of the Nineteenth Century*, Oxford, 1972

Port, M H, *Six Hundred New Churches*, London, 1961

Service, Alastair, *Edwardian Architecture and Its Origins*, London, 1975

Scott, Jonathan, *Piranesi*, London, 1975

Simpson, Duncan, *C F A Voysey, an Architect of Individuality*, London, 1979

Stamp, Gavin, *The English House 1860–1914*, London, 1980

Stroud, Dorothy, *George Dance, Architect, 1741–1825*, London, 1971

Summerson, John, *Architecture in Britain 1530–1830*, Harmondsworth, 1969

Summerson, John, *Heavenly Mansions*, London, 1949

Summerson, John *et al*, *John Soane*, London and New York, 1983

Tadgell, Christopher, *Anges-Jacques Gabriel*, London, 1978

Vidler, Alec R, *The Church in an Age of Revolution*, Harmondsworth, 1971

Watkin, David, *Thomas Hope 1769–1831 and the Neo-Classical Ideal*, London, 1968

Wiebenson, Dora, *Sources of Greek Revival Architecture*, London, 1969

LIST OF ILLUSTRATIONS

80   St Paul's, Prior Park
81   St Paul's, Prior Park, incomplete interior, Bath Reference Library, County of Avon
82   St Paul's, Prior Park, interior
83   St Philippe du Roule, Paris, interior, from E Frisch, *Jacques-Ange Gabriel*, 1912, Polytechnic of the South Bank, London
84   Claude Lorraine, *Cephalus and Procris*, 1645, National Gallery, London
85   Beckford's Walk, Lansdown, plan, Hugh Crallan
86   Islamic Pavilion, 20 Lansdown Crescent
87   Embattled Gateway, Lansdown
88   The Royal Victoria Park, plan, Bath Reference Library, County of Avon
89   The Royal Victoria Park, gateway and *cottage ornée*
90   The Royal Victoria Park, Bath Crystal Palace, Music Hall and Winter Garden, Bath Reference Library, County of Avon
91   The Abbey Cemetery, plan, Bath Reference Library, County of Avon
92   J Buckler, *The Abbey Cemetery Chapel*, 1847, Somerset Archaeological and Natural History Society *and* The Conway Library, the Courtauld Institute of Art, *London*
93   The Deepdene, Dorking, Surrey, from J C Loudon, *Encyclopedia of Cottage, Farm and Villa Architecture*, 1833, Polytechnic of the South Bank, London
94   *An Artist's Villa*, from J B Papworth, *Rural Residences*, (2nd edition), 1832, Polytechnic of the South Bank, London
95   'Watch towers common on smaller villas and farm houses in several parts of Tuscany', from J C Loudon, *Encyclopedia of Cottage, Farm and Villa Architecture*, 1833, Polytechnic of the South Bank, London
96   Spa Villa, 9 Bathwick Hill
97   Montebello, Bathwick Hill, National Monuments Record, London
98   Fiesole, Bathwick Hill
99   La Casetta and Casa Bianca, Bathwick Hill
100 The Lansdown Tower, proposed alterations, Bath Reference Library, County of Avon
101 Smallcombe Lodge, Bathwick Hill
102 Glen Avon, Sion Road
103 'A row of circular headed windows with a balcony', from J C Loudon, *Encyclopedia of Cottage, Farm and Villa Architecture*, 1833, Polytechnic of the South Bank, London
104 Temple from Prior Park, now at Rainbow Wood House
105 'Gothick Window for a Pavillion &c', from Batty Langley, *Gothic Architecture*, 1747
106 11 The Circus, windows
107 16 Brock Street, doorway
108 St Margaret's Chapel, Brock Street, doorway
109 All Saint's Chapel, Lansdown, Bath Reference Library, County of Avon

GENERAL INDEX

(architects' and artists' dates given where
known)
(entries in *italic* refer to illustrations)

BATH BUILDINGS INDEX